move up

Pre-intermediate

Teacher's Book

A

Simon Greenall

Heinemann English Language Teaching
A division of Reed Educational and Professional Publishing Limited
Halley Court, Jordan Hill, Oxford OX2 8EJ

OXFORD MADRID ATHENS PARIS FLORENCE PRAGUE SÃO PAULO
CHICAGO MELBOURNE AUCKLAND SINGAPORE TOKYO IBADAN
GABORONE JOHANNESBURG PORTSMOUTH (NH)

ISBN 0 435 29795 3

Layout by eMC Design
Cover design by Stafford & Stafford

Note to teachers
The two tests and the Practice Book Answer Key at the back of
this book may be photocopied for use in class without the prior
written permission of Heinemann English Language Teaching.
However, please note that the copyright law, which does not
normally permit multiple copying of published material, applies
to the rest of this book.

Author's acknowledgements
I am very grateful to all the people who have contributed towards the
creation of this book. My thanks are due to:
- All the teachers I have had the privilege to meet on seminars in
  many different countries and the various people who have
  influenced my work.
- Paul Ruben for producing the tapes, and the actors for their voices.
- The various schools who piloted the material.
- Simon Stafford for the stunning design of the book.
- James Hunter and Bridget Green for their careful attention to detail
  and their creative contribution.
- Clare Leeds for her careful management of the project.
- Helena Gomm for her patient and good-humored editorial input.
- And last, but by no means least, Jill, Jack, and Alex.

Acknowledgments
The authors and publishers would like to thank the following for their
kind permission to reproduce material in this book:
James Ferguson for an extract from his article "Highway to the Andes"
published in Journey Latin America's magazine *Papagaio*, Vol.6,
1993.

While every effort has been made to trace the owners of copyright
material in this book, there have been some cases when the publishers
have been unable to contact the owners. We should be grateful to hear
from anyone who recognises their copyright material and who is
unacknowledged. We shall be pleased to make the necessary amend-
ments in future editions of the book.

Printed and bound in Great Britain by Athenaeum Press Ltd.

97 98 99 00 10 9 8 7 6 5 4 3 2 1

Contents

Introduction

Course Organization

Move Up is a general English course which will take adult and young adult learners of English from elementary level to advanced level. American English is used as the model for grammar, vocabulary, spelling, and pronun-ciation, but other varieties of English are included for listening and reading practice. The course components for each level are as follows:

For the student	For the teacher
Student's Book	Teacher's Book
Practice Book	Class cassettes
	Resource Pack
	Business Resource Pack

The Student's Book has twenty teaching lessons, four Fluency lessons, and four Progress Check lessons. After every five teaching lessons there is a Fluency lesson and a Progress Check lesson to review the language covered in the preceding teaching lessons and to present new language work relevant to the grammar, functions, and topics covered so far. Within the teaching lessons, the main grammar or language functions and the most useful vocabulary are presented in boxes that allow easy access to the principal language of the lesson. This makes the focus of the lesson clearly accessible for purposes of presentation and review. Each lesson will take about 90 minutes.

The **Class cassettes** contain all the listening and sounds work in the Student's Book.

The Practice Book has twenty practice lessons corresponding to the twenty teaching lessons in the Student's Book. The Practice Book extends work done in class with the Student's Book by providing further practice in grammar, vocabulary, reading, and writing. The activities are designed for self-access work and can be used either in the class or as self-study material. Each lesson will take between 45 and 60 minutes.

The Teacher's Book contains a presentation of the course design, methodological principles, as well as detailed teaching notes. It also includes two photocopiable tests. The teaching notes for each lesson include a step-by-step guide to teaching the lesson, a discussion of some of the difficulties the learners may encounter, and more detailed methodological issues arising from the material presented. The Practice Book Answer Key is in the Teacher's Book and may be photocopied.

The Resource Packs provide additional teaching material to practice the main language points of the teaching lessons. *Move Up* is designed to be very flexible in order to meet the very different requirements of learners. There is a Resource Pack for learners of general English and a Business Resource Pack for learners with language requirements of a more professional nature.

Each pack contains a wide variety of communicative prac-tice activities in the form of photocopiable worksheets with step-by-step Teacher's Notes on the back. There is at least one activity for each lesson in the Student's Book, and the activities can be used to extend a core teaching lesson of 90 minutes from the Student's Book with an average of 30 minutes of extra material for use in the classroom. They can also be used to review specific structures, language, or vocabulary later in the course.

As well as step-by-step Teacher's Notes for each activity, each Resource Pack includes an introduction which explains how to use the worksheets and offers tips on how to get the most out of the activities.

Course Design

The course design is based on a broad and integrated multi-syllabus approach. It is broad in the sense that it covers grammar and language functions, vocabulary, reading, listening, speaking, writing, and sounds explicitly, and topics, learner training, and socio-cultural competence implicitly. It is integrated in that each strand of the course design forms the overall theme of each lesson. The lessons always include activities focusing on grammar and language functions, and vocabulary. They also include reading, listening, speaking, writing, and sounds. The inclusion of each strand of the syllabus is justified by its communicative purpose within the activity sequence. The methodological principles and approaches to each strand of course design are discussed below.

Methodological Principles

Here is an outline of the methodological principles for each strand of the course design.

Grammar and Language Functions

Many teachers and learners feel safe with grammar and language functions. Some learners may claim that they want or need grammar, although at the same time suggest that they don't enjoy it. Some teachers feel that their learners' knowledge of grammar is demonstrable proof of language acquisition. But this is only partly true. Mistakes of grammar are more easily tolerated than mistakes of vocabulary, as far as comprehension is concerned, and may be more acceptable than mistakes of socio-cultural competence, as far as behavior and effective communication is concerned. *Move Up* attempts to establish grammar and language functions in their pivotal position, but without neglecting the other strands of the multi-syllabus design.

Vocabulary

There are two important criteria for the inclusion of words in the vocabulary boxes. Firstly, they are words which the pre-intermediate learner should acquire in order to communicate successfully in a number of social or transactional situations. Secondly, they may also be words which are generated by the reading or listening material, and are considered suitable for the pre-intermediate level. However, an overriding principle operates: there is usually an activity which allows learners to focus on and, one hopes, acquire the words which are personally relevant to them. This involves a process of personal selection or grouping of words according to personal categories. It is hard to acquire words which one doesn't need, so this approach responds to the learner's individual requirements and personal motivation. *Move Up* Pre-intermediate presents approximately 950 words in the vocabulary boxes for the learner's active attention, but each learner must decide which words to focus on. The *Wordbank* in the Practice Book encourages students to store the words they need in categories which are relevant to them.

Reading

The reading passages are generally at a higher level than one might expect for learners at pre-intermediate level. Foreign language users who are not of near-native speaker competence are constantly confronted with difficult language, and to expose the learners to examples of real-life English in the reassuring context of the classroom is to help prepare them for the conditions of real life. There is always an activity or two which encourages the learner to respond to the passage either on a personal level or to focus on its main ideas. *Move Up* attempts to avoid a purely pedagogical approach to reading, and encourages the learner to respond to the reading passage in a personal and genuine way before using it for other purposes.

Listening

Listening is based on a similar approach to reading in *Move Up*. Learners are often exposed to examples of natural, authentic English in order to prepare them for real-life situations in which they will have to listen to ungraded English. But the tasks are always graded for the learners' particular level. Learners at pre-intermediate level are often pleased by how much they understand. Learners at higher levels are often disappointed by how little they understand. A number of different native and non-native accents are used in the listening passages to reflect the fact that in real life very few speakers using English speak with standard American or British pronunciation.

Speaking

Many opportunities are given for speaking, particularly in pairwork and groupwork. Learners are encouraged to work in pairs and groups because the number of learners in most classes does not allow the teacher to give undivided attention to each learner's English. In these circumstances, it is important for the teacher to evaluate whether fluency or accuracy is the most important criterion. On most occasions in *Move Up* Pre-intermediate, speaking practice in the *Grammar* sections is concerned with accuracy, and in the *Speaking* sections with fluency. In the latter sections, it is better not to interrupt and correct the learners until after the activity has finished.

Writing

The writing activities in *Move Up* are based on guided paragraph writing with work on making notes, turning notes into sentences, and joining sentences into paragraphs with various linking devices. The activities are quite tightly controlled. This is not to suggest that more creative work is not valid, but it is one of the responsibilities of a coursebook to provide a systematic grounding in the skill. More creative writing is covered in the Practice Book. Work is also done on punctuation, and most of the writing activities are based on real-life tasks, such as writing letters and cards.

Sounds

Pronunciation, stress, and intonation work tends to interrupt the communicative flow of a lesson, and there is a temptation to leave it out in the interests of maintaining the momentum of an activity sequence. In *Move Up* there is work on sounds in most lessons, usually just before the stage where the learners have to use the new structures orally in pairwork or groupwork. At this level, it seems suitable to introduce work beyond the straightforward system of English phonemes, most of which the learners will be able to reproduce accurately because the same phonemes exist in their own language. So activities which focus on stress in words and sentences, and on the implied meaning of certain intonation patterns, are included. The model for pronunciation is American English.

Topics

The main topics covered in *Move Up* Pre-intermediate include personal identification, house and home, daily life, leisure activities, travel, relations with other people, health, education, shopping, food and drink, geographical location, and the environment. On many occasions, the words presented in the vocabulary box all belong to a particular word field or topic.

Learner Training

Implicit in the overall approach is the development of learner training to encourage learners to take responsibility for their own learning. Examples of this are regular opportunities to use monolingual and bilingual dictionaries, ways of organizing vocabulary according to personal categories, and inductive grammar work.

Cross-cultural Training

Much of the material and activities in *Move Up* creates the opportunity for cross-cultural training. Most learners will be using English as a medium of communication with other non-native speakers, and certainly with people of different cultures. Errors of socio-cultural competence are likely to be less easily tolerated than errors of grammar or lexical insufficiency. But it is impossible to give the learners enough specific information about a culture because it is impossible to predict all the cultural circumstances in which they will use their newly acquired language competence. Information about *sample* cultures, such as the United States and Britain, as well as non-English speaking ones, is given to allow the learners to compare their own culture with another. This creates opportunities for learners to reflect on their own culture in order to become more aware of the possibility of different attitudes, behavior, customs, traditions, and beliefs in other cultures. In this spirit, cross-cultural training is possible even with groups where the learners all come from the same cultural background. There are interesting and revealing differences between people from the same region or town, or even between friends and members of the same family. Exploring these will help the learners become not merely proficient in the language, but competent in the overall aim of communication.

Level and Progress

One important principle behind *Move Up* is that the learners arrive at pre-intermediate level with very different language abilities and requirements. Some may find the early lessons very easy and will be able to move quickly on to later lessons. The way *Move Up* is structured, with individual lessons of approximately 90 minutes, means that these learners can confirm that they have acquired a certain area of grammar, language function, and vocabulary, consolidate this competence with activities giving practice in the other aspects of the course design, and then move on. Others may find that their previous language competence needs to be reactivated more carefully and slowly. The core teaching lesson in the Student's Book may not provide them with enough practice material to ensure that the given grammar, language functions, and vocabulary have been firmly acquired. For these learners, extra practice may be needed and is provided in both the Practice Book (for self-study work) and by the Resource Packs (for classroom work). If learners return to language training at pre-intermediate level after a long period of little or no practice, it is hard to predict what they still know. *Move Up* is designed to help this kind of learner as much as those who need to confirm that they have already acquired a basic knowledge of English.

Correction

You may need to tell your students your policy on correction. Some may expect you to correct every mistake; others will be hesitant to join in if they are nervous about correction. You need to decide when, and how often you want to correct people. Of course, this will depend on the person and the activity, but it might be worth making the distinction between activities which encourage accuracy, in which it is very suitable to provide a certain amount of correction, and activities which focus on fluency, in which it may be better to note down mistakes and give them to the student at a later stage. Another approach may be to encourage accuracy at the beginning of a practice sequence and fluency towards the end. Let them know the general principles. It will create a positive impression even for those who may, at first, disagree with it.

Interest and Motivation

Another important principle in the course design has been the intrinsic interest of the materials. Interesting material motivates the learners, and motivated learners acquire the language more effectively. The topics have been carefully selected so that they are interesting to adults and young adults, with a focus on areas which would engage their general leisure-time interests. This is designed to generate what might be described as authentic motivation, the kind of motivation we have when we read a newspaper or watch a television program. But it is obvious that we cannot motivate all learners all of the time. They may arrive at a potentially motivating lesson with little desire to learn on this particular occasion, perhaps for reasons that have nothing to do with the teacher, the course, or the material. It is therefore necessary to introduce tasks which attract what might be described as pedagogic or artificial motivation, tasks which would not usually be performed in real life, but which engage the learner in an artificial, but no less effective way.

Variety of Material and Language

Despite the enormous amount of research done on language acquisition, no one has come up with a definitive description of how we acquire either our native language or a foreign language which takes account of every language learner or the teaching style of every teacher. Every learner has different interests and different requirements, and every teacher has a different style and approach to what they teach. *Move Up* attempts to adopt an approach which appeals to differing styles of learning and teaching. The pivotal role of grammar and vocabulary is reflected in the material, but not at the expense of the development of the skills or pronunciation. An integrated multi-syllabus course design, designed to respond to the broad variety of learners' requirements and teachers' objectives, is at the heart of *Move Up's* approach.

RESEARCH

Heinemann ELT is committed to continuing research into coursebook development. Many teachers contributed to the evolution of *Move Up* through piloting and reports, and we now want to continue this process of feedback by inviting users of *Move Up*—both teachers and students—to tell us about their experience of working with the course. If you or your colleagues have any comments, questions, or suggestions, please address them to the Publisher, Adult Group, Heinemann ELT, Halley Court, Jordan Hill, Oxford OX2 8EJ or contact your local Heinemann representative.

Map of the Book

Lesson	Grammar and functions	Vocabulary	Skills and sounds
Progress Check Lessons 6–10	Review	Word chains Compound nouns Categorizing vocabulary	**Sounds:** syllable stress in words; /ð/ and /θ/; /ɒ/ and /əʊ/; friendly intonation **Writing:** predicting a story from questions **Speaking:** talking about past events; families
11 *How Ambitious Are You?* Talking about ambitions	Verb patterns (2): *to* + infinitive; *going to* for intentions, *would like to* for ambitions	Ambitions Verbs and nouns which go together	**Reading:** reading and answering a questionnaire **Writing:** writing a paragraph describing your ambitions using *because* and *so*
12 *English in the Future* The role of the English language in the future of your country	*Will* for predictions	Jobs School subjects	**Listening:** listening for main ideas **Sounds:** syllable stress in words; /e/ and /eɪ/ **Speaking:** talking about the future of English
13 *Foreign Travels* Planning a trip to South America	*Going to* for plans and *will* for decisions Expressions of future time	Equipment for travelers	**Listening:** listening for specific information **Speaking:** planning a trip
14 *All That Jazz* Finding your way around town	Prepositions of place Asking for and giving directions	Town features Adjectives to describe places	**Reading:** reacting to a passage **Listening:** listening for specific information **Sounds:** /æ/, /ə/, /ɑː/, and /eɪ/ **Speaking:** giving directions around town
15 *An Apple a Day* Typical meals in different countries	Expressions of quantity: countable and uncountable nouns, *some* and *any, much* and *many*	Food and drink Meals	**Listening:** listening for specific information **Speaking:** talking about typical meals and food in different countries

Fluency 3 *The Cost of Living* **Numbers and prices**

Lesson	Grammar and functions	Vocabulary	Skills and sounds
Progress Check Lessons 11 – 15	Review	Word maps Nouns from verbs and nouns from other nouns Noun suffixes for jobs	**Sounds:** weak syllables /ə/; /tʃ/, and /ʃ/; contrastive stress; polite intonation in questions **Speaking:** planning a lunch party for friends
16 *What's On?* Typical entertainment in different countries	Prepositions of time and place Making invitations and suggestions	Types and places of entertainment and related words	**Listening:** listening for specific information **Speaking:** talking about typical entertainment **Writing:** writing and replying to invitations
17 *Famous Faces* Describing people	Describing appearance and character: *look like, be like*	Words to describe height, age, looks, build, and character	**Speaking:** describing people **Writing:** writing a letter describing your appearance
18 *Average Age* Personal qualities at different ages	Making comparisons (1): comparative and superlative adjectives	Adjectives of character	**Reading:** reacting to a passage and comparing information in a passage with your own experience **Speaking:** talking about exceptional people **Writing:** writing sentences describing exceptional people
19 *Dressing Up* Typical clothes in different countries	Making comparisons (2): *more than, less than, as ... as*	Clothes Colors Personal categories for organizing new vocabulary	**Reading:** reading for specific information **Sounds:** weak syllables /ə/; weak forms /ðən/, /əz/, and /frəm/; stress for disagreement **Listening:** listening for main ideas **Speaking:** talking about clothing
20 *Memorable Journeys* A car journey across the United States	Talking about journey time, distance, speed, and prices	Numbers Words to describe a long-distance journey by car	**Listening:** listening for specific information **Sounds:** syllable stress in numbers **Speaking:** talking about a memorable journey

Fluency 4 *Special Occasions* **Saying dates; saying the right thing**

Lesson	Grammar and functions	Vocabulary	Skills and sounds
Progress Check Lessons 16 – 20	Review	International words Adjective suffixes Male and female words	**Sounds:** /ʊ/ and /uː/; /dʒ/; polite and friendly intonation **Speaking:** pair dictation **Writing:** pair dictation to recreate a story

1

GENERAL COMMENTS

Beginning the course

It may be that at the start of the course, the students need to get to know each other. In *Speaking and Listening* there are a number of activities which give the students the necessary language and opportunities to introduce themselves to each other. At this stage, most people will be unfamiliar with the coursebook and may be unsure of the reasons why they are doing certain activities. Be ready to explain anything which the students may be unsure about.

SPEAKING AND LISTENING

1. Aim: to present some common words and phrases for greetings and simple transactions; to make a simple distinction between transactional and social situations.

- Write the situations on the board and ask the students to write the expressions under the situations.

> **Possible Answers**
> **in a bar:** Can I help you? How much is this?
>   Thank you. I'd like a Coca Cola.
> **in a store:** Hello. Goodbye. Can I help you?
>   How much is this? Thank you. I'd like a
>   Coca Cola.
> **in a hotel:** Hello. Goodbye. Can I help you?
>   Thank you.
> **at home:** Hello. Goodbye. Come in. Pleased to
>   meet you. Thank you. Fine, thanks. Sorry!
>   How are you? This is my friend, Rosario.
> **in class:** Hello. Goodbye. Pleased t11o meet you.
>   Thank you. I don't understand. Could you
>   repeat that?

2. Aim: to practice listening for main ideas.

- Explain that the students are going to listen to two dialogues. They should guess the situation of each dialogue from the five given in activity 1. Tell them not worry if they don't understand every word.

- [cassette] Play the cassette.

> **Answers**
> Situation 1: at home, Situation 2: in a bar

- Elicit the correct answers. Try to resist explaining the meaning of individual words. Explain that the aim of the activity was to listen for main ideas.

3. Aim: to focus on word order in questions.

- Explain that the words are in the wrong order and the task is to put them in the right order and make questions.

- You may like to elicit the correct word stress. Explain that usually the words which are stressed are those which the speaker considers to be important.

- [cassette] Play the cassette.

> **Answers**
> 1. What's your first name?
> 2. Where do you live?
> 3. Are you married?
> 4. What do you do?
> 5. Do you have any brothers and sisters?
> 6. Where do you come from?

4. Aim: to practice the language presented so far in this lesson.

- Ask the students to go around the class using the words and phrases in *Speaking and Listening* activity 1.

READING

1. Aim: to encourage the students to read for main ideas; to discourage them from trying to understand every word.

- Explain that the paragraphs give some very general information about customs of hospitality in different countries. The information is offered as a guide, not as a set of rules.

- Ask the students to read and match the headings with the paragraphs. Try not to explain too much vocabulary. If necessary, tell the students that you will explain the meaning of six words only, and they must choose these words carefully.

- When they have read the passage once on their own, ask them to work in pairs and to check their answers. Encourage them to help each other with any difficult vocabulary.

> **Answers**
> a. **special customs:** paragraph 1, Japan
> b. **refreshments:** paragraph 2, Saudi Arabia
> c. **length of stay:** paragraph 3, U.S.A.
> d. **time of arrival:** paragraph 4, U.S.A.

2. Aim: to compare other people's cultures with the students' own culture.

- Ask the students to compare the situations they have read about with similar situations in their own culture. It may be that they belong to one of the countries mentioned. If so, ask them if they think the information given in the passage is accurate. If they think it isn't accurate, ask them to correct it.

GRAMMAR

1. Aim: to focus on verbs in the present simple.
- Tell the students that the grammar focus of this lesson is the present simple. Ask them to look at the passage again and find some verbs in the present simple. Ask them to make new sentences with these verbs. Suggest that they talk about customs and traditions of hospitality in their own country.

- Ask the students to guess what the missing verb might be. Then suggest that they check to see if the verb is in the passage. Take this opportunity to point out that they can often guess the general sense of a difficult word by looking for clues in the context.

- Ask if anyone knows when to use the present simple.

- Ask them to read the explanation about the present simple in the grammar box.

Answers
1. sit 2. arrive 3. drink / leave 4. go

2. Aim: to focus on present simple questions.
- Write *who, what, where* on the board and ask the students to suggest other question words. Ask the students to use the words in questions.

- Ask the students to do the exercise.

Possible Answers
a. What do you wear to a dinner party?
b. How long do you stay?
c. What do you have to eat or drink?
d. Are there any special customs? *or*
   What special customs are there?
e. What gifts do you take?
f. What do you talk about? *or*
   What topics of conversation do you never talk about?
g. What time/When do you arrive?

3. Aim: to focus on adverbs of frequency.
- Ask the students to look at the adverbs of frequency in the grammar box and to make sentences using each one.

- Ask them to read the explanation about adverbs of frequency in the grammar box.

Answers
Para 1: usually go, always take, usually sit, often sing
Para 2: always offer, always stay
Para 3: often lasts, is sometimes
Para 4: never arrive

WRITING AND VOCABULARY

1. Aim: to focus on some key vocabulary from this lesson; to practice writing sentences in the present simple.
- Explain that the vocabulary boxes in *Move Up* contain the most important vocabulary in the lesson.

- Ask the students to use the vocabulary to write seven or eight sentences about customs of hospitality in their country. They may like to do this in pairs. Remind them to insert adverbs of frequency into their sentences.

2. Aim: to practice joining sentences into a paragraph.
- Ask the students to write a single sentence in answer to the questions they wrote in *Grammar* activity 2.

- Write up two sentences on the board, side by side, and link them with *and* or *but* to make a paragraph.

- Ask the students to join their sentences and make paragraphs. You may like to ask them to do this for homework.

2

GENERAL COMMENTS

Many students start reading or listening to a passage and then stop because they don't understand a particular word. Many reading and listening activity sequences in *Move Up* begin with a task to encourage the students to extract the main ideas. This is designed not only to help them gain access to the heart of the passage but also to help them overlook any difficult words. If you explain every word, you may help extend the students' vocabulary, but you will not help them to become more effective readers. If you do need to explain words, limit them to five or six and ask the class to choose them carefully. Explain also that the vocabulary in the boxes is the vocabulary which is considered suitable for this level. Other words are less important. Finally, point out that it is difficult to learn more than ten or twelve words a lesson, and simply noting down more will not make the learning process more efficient.

READING AND VOCABULARY

1. **Aim: to practice reading for main ideas.**
- Explain that the passage the students are going to read is about a typical day in the life of some Americans. Before they begin, write these words on the board: *breakfast, station, train, meeting, lunch, woman, swim, aerobics, bar, dinner, TV, children*

- Pre-teach these words which come from the passage by asking the students to say which ones they can use to describe what they can see in the photos.

- Ask the students to read the passage and decide who they can see in the photos.

> **Answers**
> Top: Possibly Amelia Noriega and friend or Jo-Ann Rosenthal and friend, bottom: Cliff Renton and Walt Avery

2. **Aim: to practice saying times of the day.**
- Write the actual time on the board and ask your students how many ways they can say it in their language. Explain that there are two ways of saying the time in English, and that it isn't common to use the twenty-four hour clock in American English except for military timetables. You can also mention that the afternoon begins after noon, the evening after six P.M., and night at about ten or eleven P.M.

- Ask them to write the times in the passage in two different ways.

- Explain that you can use the present continuous to describe actions which are going on at or around a particular time, and that the present continuous will be covered in Lesson 5.

- Ask the students to work in pairs and ask and say what they do at the different times mentioned.

3. **Aim: to present the verbs and nouns in the boxes and to focus on collocations.**
- Explain that certain verbs are often followed by certain nouns. There may be many possible combinations, but here are the most common routine activities.

> **Possible Answers**
> **start:** breakfast, dinner, lunch, school, work
> **finish:** breakfast, dinner, lunch, school, work
> **come:** home
> **get:** home, breakfast, dinner, lunch
> **leave:** home, school, work
> **have:** breakfast, dinner, lunch
> **stop:** work
> **watch:** television

4. **Aim: to present the vocabulary items in the box; to practice saying the time.**
- Present the items of vocabulary in the box by saying when you do the routine activities. Write *When do you...?* on the board. Ask questions and elicit answers from two or three students.

- Ask the students to work in pairs and to ask and answer questions about the routine activities.

GRAMMAR

1. **Aim: to focus on the form of the third person singular in the present simple.**

● Explain that the focus of this lesson is on the third person singular (*he/she/it* form) of the present simple. Ask the students to think of an activity they do as a routine every week, month, or year.

● Ask the students to write down the third person singular of the verbs. Then ask them to check their answers by re-reading the passage.

● Ask the students to read the explanation about the present simple: third person singular in the grammar box.

Answers
comes, drives, joins, finishes, gets, hurries, leaves, meets, says, stops, takes, teaches, tries, walks, washes, watches, works

2. **Aim: to focus on the three endings of the third person singular in the present simple.**

● Explain that there are three endings for the third person singular of the present simple. Draw three columns on the board and ask the students to suggest where each verb should go.

Answers
-s: comes, drives, joins, gets, leaves, meets, says, stops, takes, walks, works, lives, makes
-es: goes, finishes, teaches, washes, watches, does, dresses
-ies: hurries, tries, flies, carries

LISTENING

1. **Aim: to practice listening for main ideas.**

● 🔲 Explain to the students that they are going to listen to two people from *A Day in the Life of the U.S.A.* talking some more about their typical days. Remind them that it isn't necessary to understand every word. Ask them to listen and decide who is speaking. Play the cassette.

Answers
First person: Jo-Ann Rosenthal
Second person: George Markopoulos

2. **Aim: to practice listening for specific information.**

● 🔲 Ask the students to listen again and find out what they are doing at the specific times mentioned. Play the tape.

Answers
Jo-Ann: 8 A.M.: leaves home and goes to work; 1 P.M.: takes a walk in the park; 5:00 P.M.: leaves work; 11:30 P.M.: goes to bed.
George: 8:15 A.M.: has breakfast; 12:30 P.M.: has lunch; 5:30 P.M.: meets friends and has a drink at the golf club; 7 P.M.: goes home for dinner.

3. **Aim: to practice saying the time and using verbs in the third person singular.**

● Ask the students to check their answers to activity 2. Make sure that everyone is using and pronouncing the endings correctly.

SOUNDS

1. **Aim: to show ways of pronouncing the letter *s* as an ending for the third person singular present simple; to practice pronouncing /s/, /z/, and /ɪz/.**

● Write /s/, /z/, and /ɪz/ on the board and say each sound. Point to each sound in turn and ask the class to say the sound. You may like to draw the students' attention to the Pronunciation guide at the back of the book.

● Write 1, 2, and 3 by the three sounds. Ask the students to listen and write 1, 2, or 3 according to the sound they hear.

● 🔲 Play the tape.

● Ask the students to write the words in the correct columns.

2. **Aim: to check answers to activity 1; to practice pronouncing /s/, /z/, and /ɪz/.**

● 🔲 Play the tape.

Answers
/s/: takes sits asks talks
/z/: goes sings arrives offers has serves does
/ɪz/: finishes refuses washes watches

● Ask the students to say the words out loud as a group, and then in pairs. If necessary, play the tape and stop after every word so they can repeat it.

SPEAKING

Aim: to practice asking and answering questions about routine activities.

● Ask the students to find out when their partner does the five routine activities mentioned. Check that everyone is using the auxiliary *do*.

3

GENERAL COMMENTS

Articles

The explanation in the grammar box about the use of articles is brief for reasons of space. Your students will probably have already been exposed to how articles are used in English, and the explanation should be seen as consolidation. You may need to remind them that *an* is used before words beginning with a vowel sound. However, they may need more practice, especially if the English article is used in different ways in their own language.

Plurals

The general rule for forming plurals in English by adding *-s* is fairly straightforward, and the exceptions are few. It may sometimes be difficult to decide if a word is plural or singular. For example, *hair, police, news,* and *money* are uncountable nouns (see Lesson 15) and therefore take singular verb forms. This aspect of the word needs to be taught at the time the item is first presented.

Optional extra material

It would be helpful for the early stages of *Vocabulary* activity 1 if you used magazine photos of items of furniture, household equipment, or rooms of the house.

VOCABULARY

1. **Aim: to present the vocabulary items in the box and to prepare the students for the reading passage.**

● Tell the students that the subject of the lesson is homes. Review present simple questions by asking them:
Where do you live?
Do you live in an apartment or a house?
Do you live in town or in the country?

● Point to some items of furniture and equipment in the classroom and ask the students: *What's this?* Find out how many words to do with houses they know. Use the photo to present the vocabulary items.

● Write *types of housing* and *rooms* on the board. Ask the students to look at the vocabulary box and find two types of housing and six rooms.

> **Answers**
> **types of housing:** apartment, house
> **rooms:** bathroom, bedroom, dining room, kitchen, living room

2. **Aim: to continue the presentation of the vocabulary items in the box and the process of categorization.**

● Ask the students to put the words for furniture and equipment with the rooms. You may be able to do this very effectively with extra magazine photos. Some items may go in more than one room.

> **Possible Answers**
> **bathroom:** bath, shower, sink, toilet
> **bedroom:** bed, carpet, chair, closet, drapes, lamp, table
> **dining room:** carpet, chair, drapes, lamp, table
> **living room:** carpet, chair, drapes, lamp, sofa, table, video
> **kitchen:** dishwasher, refrigerator, sink, stove, table, washing machine

● Write *yard* on the board and explain that it does not fit in the categories. *Door* and *window* fit all the rooms. Check that everyone knows what the words mean by using photos, drawings, or pointing.

3. **Aim: to practice using the vocabulary in the box with *Is there...?***

● Write *Yes, there is* and *No, there isn't* on the board. Ask one or two students a few questions: *Is there a living room in your home? Is there a dining room?* Point to the replies on the board and ask them to reply. Make sure they reply using the full sentence.

● Ask the students to work in pairs and to continue asking and answering questions about their homes.

● Ask one or two students about what furniture and equipment there is in the rooms of their home. The answers may be different from the answers in activity 2. Make sure that if they use a plural noun in reply, they also say *Yes, there are two/three chairs.*

● Ask the students to work in pairs and write down what furniture and equipment there is in the different rooms. Encourage them to expand their lists with vocabulary of their own choice at this stage.

READING

Aim: to practice reading for specific information; to react to the text.

● Ask them to read *Home at Last* and think about their answers to the questions. Suggest that they make notes at this stage, which they will use in *Speaking* activity 2.

GRAMMAR

1. Aim: to focus on the use of the article in English.

● Ask the students what the articles in English are, and if they have articles in their own language.

● Ask the students to read the explanation about articles in the grammar box. While they are doing this, write the nine uses of the article from the grammar box on the board and number them.

● Ask the students to look at the nine underlined words or expressions and decide which use of the article each example shows. They should put a number by it according to the use of the article. Make it clear that there is an example of every use of the article, definite, indefinite, and zero, in the passage.

> **Answers**
> **indefinite article**
> 1. – to talk about something for the first time: *a visitor*
> 2. – with jobs: *I'm an architect*
> 3. – with certain expressions of quantity: *a lot*
> **definite article**
> 4. – to talk about something again: *we left the door open*
> 5. – with certain places and place names: *the Elburz mountains*
> 6. – when there is only one: in *the center of New York*
> **no article**
> 7. – with plural and uncountable nouns: *we love cars*
> 8. – with certain expressions: *in bed*
> 9. – with meals, languages, most countries, and most towns: *we have breakfast, lunch, and dinner*

● The explanation in the grammar box covers the rules which the students need to learn at their present level.

2. Aim: to focus on the use of the article.

● Ask the students to do this activity and to think about which uses each sentence shows.

> **Answers**
> 1. Last year we moved to – Los Angeles.
> 2. **The** kitchen is **the** door on your left.
> 3. **The** weather is very hot in August.
> 4. There isn't **a** table in **the** kitchen.
> 5. Would you like **a** drink?
> 6. I'm sorry, he's still at – work.

3. Aim: to focus on the formation of plurals.

● Ask the students if they know how to form plurals in English. Write a few simple words on the board and ask the students to tell you the plural form.

● Ask the students to read the explanation about plurals in the grammar box.

> **Answers**
> parents houses cities families dishes parties bushes countries tables faxes features

SPEAKING

1. Aim: to give practice in using the vocabulary and grammar presented so far in this lesson.

● Ask the students what room they think the photo shows, and if it looks like a room in their country. If it doesn't, can they explain why?

> **Answer**
> The photo shows a kitchen in a house in the United States. It serves as a living room too. The kitchen is usually the main room in the house.

2. Aim: to check that the students have understood the passage and have reacted to it.

● Ask one or two students to talk about their answers to the questions in the passage. In a mono-cultural group, it is likely everyone will have similar answers. Ask them if they find anything surprising or strange about the answers of the people quoted in the passage. In a multi-cultural group, encourage the students to discuss any similarities and differences.

3. Aim: to give further speaking practice and to examine attitudes towards homes.

● Write words which you associate with *home* on the board. Here are some ideas: *love, dinner, family, sleep.*

● Ask the students to write down words which they associate with *home*. Explain that they should not write the first words which come to mind but should choose their words carefully. Give them two or three minutes for this stage of the activity.

● Ask the students to share their words and phrases with the rest of the class. Once again, are there any words or phrases which people find surprising or strange?

4

GENERAL COMMENTS

Verb patterns (1): -ing form verbs

In *Move Up*, common constructions with verbs are referred to as *verb patterns*. In *Move Up* Pre-intermediate there are two verb patterns, in this lesson and in Lesson 11. When there are two verbs in a sequence, the second verb in the sequence is either an infinitive or an *-ing* form. This lesson focuses on the *-ing* form. Some students may already know that with *love, like,* and *hate,* the three main verbs presented in this lesson, you can put either *-ing* or an infinitive. If the question arises, explain that there is not much difference between the two patterns with these verbs, although if you are talking about a particular occasion, you usually use an infinitive. The most common expression is with *would like to: Would you like to go to the movies tonight?*

Talking about likes and dislikes

A very common *-ing* form verb pattern is talking about likes and dislikes. The replies presented in this lesson are graded from strong to weak likes or dislikes, so the student has a suitable range of language to reply honestly to the questions. The lesson also focuses on short answers when two people have the same or different likes and dislikes.

Cross-cultural awareness

The passage is a collection of impressions about Britain and the United States. Obviously, they can be used at face value to stimulate a discussion about the two countries and how they appear to people from other cultures. But they should also be used as an opportunity to compare Britain and the United States with the students' own cultures and countries, and to raise their awareness of how people see their own and other countries. The key to cross-cultural awareness is to develop a sensitivity towards one's own culture.

Photos: Hyde Park in London; a truck outside a motel in the United States.

READING AND VOCABULARY

1. Aim: to practice reading and inferring; to encourage the students to react to the passage.

● When we read, the meaning is not always transparently clear, and this activity encourages the students to read between the lines. The impressions that the people have about Britain and the United States are in the form of noun objects or *-ing* form verbs. *Claude likes the police, Moon likes feeling safe in the streets.* Ask the students what impressions they have of Britain and the United States. It doesn't matter if they have never been there.

● Write a few impressions on the board. If someone has given an impression without ever having been to the country, ask them where they think the impression comes from. Mention that our impressions of other countries are not simply formed by direct experience but by different sources, such as films, books, and television. Our impressions of another country may be fashioned by one or two influential sources.

● Ask the students to read the passage and decide if the impressions are positive or negative. Ask them also to compare these impressions with their own.

> **Answers**
> **Britain**
> > **positive:** the police, feeling safe, polite drivers
> > **negative:** the weather, the tourists, the litter, driving on the left
> **United States**
> > **positive:** the people, going shopping
> > **negative:** arriving at the airport, the insects, driving on the right

● Although it is helpful to draw attention to similarities between cultures, it is less remarkable than focusing on the differences. Anything which is surprising, strange, amusing, interesting, or even shocking about a culture is generally a difference. For example, like Paula, some students may find it strange that the British drive on the left-hand side of the road. Encourage the students to respond with their own reactions to the passage.

2. Aim: to present the words in the vocabulary box and to show that the meaning of words may change according to the context.

● It may be useful to help the students distinguish between parts of speech at this stage of the course since this skill becomes increasingly useful as the course continues. If necessary, they can use a dictionary.

● Start by asking the students to suggest which are the adjectives, and write them on the board.

● Ask the students if the adjectives are positive or negative according to the speakers and ask them to write the words in two columns.

● Point out that the meaning of the adjectives can change according to the context. For example, *They sell cheap clothes for children* is positive, but not *She wears cheap clothes*.

● Ask the students to remember which nouns the adjectives go with in the passage. Developing an awareness of collocation, of which words can go together, is important for two reasons. It helps the process of acquiring the vocabulary items, and it helps develop the students' vocabulary in general. Do this orally, without letting them look back at the passage.

● Ask the students to look at the passage to check which nouns the adjectives went with.

3. **Aim: to continue the presentation of the words in the vocabulary box.**
● You may like to draw attention to the words which end in *-ing* and the nouns. The *-ing* form verbs are in fact gerunds, which are verbs that act like nouns.

● Ask the students to check the things they like and put a cross by the things they dislike. In theory, they cannot answer the questions yet, as they have not read the grammar and functions box. However, it may be that the students are in fact reviewing this structure, so you may like to ask questions like *Do you like the beach? Do you like the countryside?* and elicit a suitable short answer *Yes, I do* or *No I don't.*

GRAMMAR AND FUNCTIONS

1. **Aim: to practice saying if you have the same likes and dislikes as other people.**
● Ask the students to read the information about verb patterns and talking about likes and dislikes in the grammar and functions box.

● Ask the students to respond truthfully to these statements. You may like to do this activity orally.

2. **Aim: to check the students' answers to *Reading and Vocabulary* activity 1 and to practice saying the full sentences with *like* and *dislike*.**
● It may be easier to do this activity orally. Remind the students that the ✔ sign they wrote by each impression means they must use *likes* and the ✗ sign means they must use *dislikes*. Make sure the students pronounce the third person singular ending correctly. (See Lesson 2 for more information.) Encourage them also to use full sentences with *because*.

SOUNDS

Aim: to focus on the use of intonation to show strong likes and dislikes.
● Explain that intonation can be used to show strong likes or dislikes. All the sentences have a strong intonation. Usually, the key word is heavily stressed, and this has an effect on the intonation pattern which follows. Ask the students if they think their own language has similar intonation patterns for strong likes and dislikes.

● 🔲 Play the tape.

● 🔲 Play the tape again and stop after each sentence. Ask the students to say the sentences out loud. Make sure they use strong intonation.

● Ask the students for other likes and dislikes using strong intonation.

SPEAKING

1. **Aim: to encourage the students to think about what they like and dislike about their town or country, or the town where they are now.**
● Ask the students to work alone and write down things they like and dislike about their town or country, or the town where they are now. This is a good opportunity to prepare for the discussion of cross-cultural comparisons mentioned in the *General Comments* at the beginning of these notes. You may need to help them at this stage with vocabulary.

2. **Aim: to practice talking about likes and dislikes.**
● Think of something you like, such as going shopping and go around asking the students *Do you like going shopping?* Ask the students to do the same. When they have found someone who likes the same things, ask them to find things they both dislike. If your classroom doesn't allow much room for students to move around, they can do this activity with their close neighbors.

3. **Aim: to continue talking about likes and dislikes.**
● Ask the students about their likes and dislikes, and write them on the board. Some people may like things which other people dislike. Use this as an opportunity to point out that even within our own culture there are different likes and dislikes, and that this should help the students be more aware of differences in other cultures.

● Try to get the class to rank the likes and dislikes in two *Top Five* lists. This kind of ranking activity is very effective for stimulating discussion.

● You may like to ask the students to find out about the likes and dislikes of their family and friends, and to write a few sentences in English using the passage in this lesson as a model.

5

GENERAL COMMENTS

Present continuous

This tense is also called the *present progressive* because it can be used to describe activities which are in progress at the time of speaking as well as repeated or continuous actions. It can also be used to talk about a future situation: *What are you doing this weekend? I'm staying at home.* There are two possible points of confusion. Firstly, many languages do not have a progressive aspect to their tense system and speakers of these languages may often have some trouble distinguishing it from the present simple. Secondly, the present participle has the same form as the gerund, although it has a very different function. It may be useful to point out that, for example, the word *smoking* in *I'm smoking a cigarette* does not have the same function as the same word in *smoking is bad for you.* Your students may also have problems with word order in questions, for example, *Why is standing the woman there?* Most students will already have come across the difference between the present simple and continuous tenses, so this lesson should to a large extent be review.

Photos

The photos in this lesson were taken by the French photographer Robert Doisneau, whose most famous photograph is *The Kiss.* It is common to use the present continuous to describe what is happening in a photograph, picture, or scene, maybe to someone who cannot see it.

SPEAKING

1. **Aim: to review the present simple and to create an opportunity to compare it with the present continuous later in the lesson.**
- This activity will work best if your students know each other a little, but not well. You may want to separate those who know each other well, and ask them to work with people they know less well. If this is not possible, the questions are sufficiently varied to generate a meaningful question and answer exchange in activity 2. (If a student knows that his or her partner plays a musical instrument, it isn't meaningful to ask the question!)

- Say and write on the board what you think one or two students in the class do: *I think Akira plays the piano. I think Maria works hard.* Ask the students *What about me?* and get them to think about you the teacher, and how you might answer the questions. Ask the students to write their guesses on the board.

- Ask them to work in pairs with people they don't know well and to guess the answers to the questions.

2. **Aim: to practice asking and answering questions using the present simple.**
- Ask one or two students the questions: *Akira, do you play the piano? Maria, do you work hard?* and get them to say *yes* or *no.* Then get the students to ask their questions about you and give suitable answers.

- Ask the students to continue the activity, asking and answering the questions in activity 1 about themselves. Remind the students that they are using the present simple to ask and talk about habits, personal characteristics, and general truths.

- Find out who guessed correctly in activity 1.

3. **Aim: to present the main difference between the present simple and the present continuous.**
- Write *at the moment?* on the board and ask the questions, using the present continuous but pointing to and stressing *at the moment.*

4. **Aim: to focus on the present simple as preparation for its comparison with the present continuous.**
- Ask the students to think about the people in the photos. Ask these questions.
Where are they? What town are they in? When was the photo taken?

- Ask the students to answer the questions in *Speaking* activity 1 about the people in the photos.

GRAMMAR

1. **Aim: to present or review present continuous questions and affirmative statements.**
- Ask the students to read about the present simple and present continuous in the grammar box.

- Ask the students to work in pairs. Ask *What's the man in front doing?* and find someone who gives a suitable answer using the present continuous. Ask several more questions like this and obtain suitable answers, using vocabulary from the list in the Student's Book. Write *What is doing the man in front?* on the board, cross it out and rewrite it correctly.

- Ask the students questions with *why. Why is he playing the accordion? Why is he drawing?* and elicit suitable answers. Go around the class asking students to form questions with the correct word order.

- Ask the students to work in pairs and to ask and say what the people in the photos are doing, and why.

2. **Aim: to focus on the formation of present participles.**
- Orally, this activity does not pose great problems. It is only when you start to write the present participles that the issue of correct spelling arises. This activity shows the students the present participle, asks them to write down the information they know already, which is the infinitive form, and then reflect on the possible rules for forming the present continuous endings.

Answers

draw, get, have, make, play, shop, put, stay
With infinitives:
– ending in -e: you drop the -e and add -ing.
– ending in -t and -p: you double the consonant and
  add -ing.
– ending in -y: you add -ing.

● It may be a suitable moment to explain that this is a
very general rule, and that more complete information
can be found in the Grammar Review.

3. Aim: to focus on the difference between the
present simple and present continuous in
sentences using *and* and *but*.
  ● Ask the students to complete the sentences.

Answers

1. I often go shopping at the supermarket **and** I'm
   going there now.
2. They usually eat at home **but** today they're
   having dinner in a restaurant.
3. She walks to work **but** this week she's taking the bus.
4. He smokes ten cigarettes a day **but** he's smoking
   a cigar right now.

SOUNDS

Aim: to practice the sounds /n/ and /ŋ/.
● Read each phrase out loud so the students can hear
the difference.

● 📻 Play the tape and repeat each phrase.

Answers

1. carryi*ng* an umbrella   4. arrive *in* time
2. sitti*ng* there   5. taki*ng* money
3. si*ng in* tune   6. stand *in* there

● Play the tape again, stopping after each phrase. Ask
the students to say the phrases out loud.

LISTENING AND VOCABULARY

1. Aim: to prepare for the listening activity in 2.
  ● Ask the students to match the things with the places.
Remind them to use the present simple tense for
general truths, for example, *You buy plane tickets at
the travel agent.*

Answers

buy plane tickets: at the travel agency
have dinner: in a restaurant
change money: in a bank
get some medicine: at a drugstore
buy food: at a grocery store

2. Aim: to expose the students to some natural
language in transactional situations, and to
encourage them to listen for main ideas; to give
further practice in using the present continuous.

● 📻 The level of language in this activity is quite
high, but the task is very simple and is designed to
distract the students from trying to understand every
single word. Explain that they need to be exposed to
real-life English in the classroom context in order to
prepare themselves for listening in a real-life context.
They won't understand every word, but then they
wouldn't in real life either. Explain that the task is to
listen and decide where the people are.

Answers

Conversation 1: in a bank
Conversation 2: in a restaurant
Conversation 3: at a travel agency
Conversation 4: at a drugstore

● Check the students' answers to the activity by asking
them where people are and what they are doing.

● If there were difficulties over choosing the correct
preposition in the answers to this activity, explain that
more work will be done on this in Lesson 16.

3. Aim: to present the words in the vocabulary box
and to discuss their parts of speech.
  ● Ask the students to say if the words in the box are
nouns or verbs, or both. You may like to take this opportunity to show them the dictionary entries for some of
these words. This may be the first time they have used
dictionaries, so take plenty of time for this activity.

Answers

bank *n* and *v*   bus *n* and *v*   buy *v* and *n*
change *n* and *v*   close *n* and *v*   cross *n* and *v*
draw *n* and *v*   food *n*   get *v*   grocery store *n*
hold *n* and *v*   line *n* and *v*   look at *v*   medicine *n*
money *n*   paint *n* and *v*   pharmacist *n*   play *n* and *v*
post office *n*   put *v*   railroad station *n*   rain *n* and *v*
road *n*   shelter *n* and *v*   shop *n* and *v*   sit *v*
stand *n* and *v*   stay *n* and *v*   street *n*   suitcase *n*
take *n* and *v*   think *v*   ticket *n*   town *n*   umbrella *n*
wait for *v*   walk *n* and *v*

4. Aim: to continue the presentation of the
vocabulary items in the box and to develop
an awareness of words which go together.
  ● Ask the students to group any words which go together. This type of activity encourages the students to
group the new vocabulary in word fields. It can be very
effective to get them to choose their own word fields,
although with concrete words like those in the vocabulary box, the fields are likely to be fairly predictable.

● It may be a suitable moment to draw the students'
attention to the multi-part verbs *look at* and *wait for*,
and put them in a special section of the *Wordbank*,
which is at the back of their Practice Books. A full
explanation of how multi-word verbs work is given
in Book B, Progress Check 11–15.

Fluency 1

GENERAL COMMENTS

The Fluency lessons in the *Move Up* series focus on developing the learners' awareness of socio-cultural similarities and differences in behavior, attitudes, customs, traditions, and beliefs. It should be clear what we can and can't expect our learners to do. We can expect them to acquire information about a foreign culture, usually the United States. We can help them become aware that an "error" of socio-cultural competence may be less well tolerated than a grammatical mistake and that this may lead to a communication breakdown. We can also hope they will have the chance to think about their own cultural identity. We can hope to make them aware that behavior in their own culture may not be automatically transferable to another cultural context. We can hope to provide them with the linguistic tools to enquire about possible differences. But we cannot expect them to acquire culture-specific information about all the different cultural contexts in which they are likely to use their newly acquired language competence. We should not expect them to "behave like Americans" when they speak English. Their own cultural identity should remain intact; it is only their awareness and tolerance of other cultures, and their ability to be effective communicators, which are the aims of the training.

This lesson has for its subject the socio-cultural aspects of behavior in the classroom.

LISTENING AND READING

1. **Aim: to encourage students to react to a dialogue.**
- This dialogue contains some questions and statements which you wouldn't normally expect to hear in the United States, but which may be heard in different cultures around the world. For example, *Have you eaten?* is a common expression in China and Hong Kong. Some cultures would not expect to use the teacher's first name. Some teachers would encourage learners to ask questions while the lesson is taking place, and others only at the end of the lesson. Many students are surprised when they're asked to work in pairs.

- Ask the students to read the dialogue and then to decide if they would hear it in a classroom in their country. Ask them if they notice anything peculiar about it. They should underline anything which they wouldn't hear in a classroom in their country.

2. **Aim: to practice speaking.**
- Ask the students to check their answers to 1 in pairs. Ask them to explain why they wouldn't hear the sentences they underlined.

3. **Aim: to practice listening for specific information.**
- 🔲 Play the tape and ask the students to cross out anything they don't hear.

Answers	
KELLY	Hello, Joe. How are you? ~~Have you eaten?~~
JOE	Hi, Kelly. Fine thanks. ~~Yes, I've eaten.~~ Hey, you look great today! That's a beautiful dress.
KELLY	Thanks. How was your weekend?
JOE	OK.
TEACHER	Good morning, everyone. My name is Steve Smith. You can call me Steve. How are you all today?
JOE	Hi Steve! We're all fine.
KELLY	Good morning, Mr. Smith. ~~Very well, thank you.~~
TEACHER	Please sit down, everyone. ~~Isn't it a beautiful day?~~
DAVE	Oh, I'm sorry I'm late. ~~Excuse me!~~
TEACHER	No problem, we've just started. Now, take out your textbooks and turn to page 15. ~~No talking please.~~
JOE	Can I ask a question? Can you tell me what *Buenos dias* means?
TEACHER	~~I'll answer your questions later.~~ It means *Good day* or *Hello* in Spanish. OK, I'd like you to work in pairs.
DAVE	~~Oh, not again.~~ Is it OK if I work with you, Kelly?
KELLY	Yes, of course.

- When they have done this, they now have a dialogue which would be quite acceptable in the United States, although not necessarily elsewhere in the world.

4. **Aim: to practice speaking.**
- Ask the students to act out the dialogue they heard in groups of four.

FUNCTIONS

1. Aim: to present the language used for greeting people.
- Ask the students to read the information in the functions box about greeting people and then to do the activity in pairs. You may like to do these activities in writing, or orally with the group as a whole.

- Use this activity as discussion for the whole class. Write up the ways of greeting people in the students' language in the classroom and see if there are any direct equivalents in English.

2. Aim: to present the language used for greeting people.
- Ask the students to say if the language they use for greeting people in other classes is more or less formal than the language they use in the English class.

3. Aim: to check the students know the English alphabet.
- Remind them that English has 26 letters.

4. Aim: to practice saying the alphabet.
- 🔊 Play the tape and ask the students to repeat the letters.

5. Aim: to practice the sounds of the alphabet.
- Ask the students to put the letters in the right column according to the phoneme.

- 🔊 Play the tape and ask the students to check their answers.

Answer

/eɪ/	/iː/		/e/
AHJK	BCDEGPTVZ		FLMNSX

/aɪ/	/əʊ/	/juː/	/aː/
IY	O	QUW	R

6. Aim: to practice using polite classroom language.
- Ask the students to read the information about asking for information in the classroom and then match the two parts of the exchange.

Answers
1. e 2. c 3. a 4. b 5. d

READING AND LISTENING

1. Aim: to practice reading and answering a questionnaire.
- The questionnaire focuses on classroom behavior. You may find that your students come from a learning culture which is much more passive or formal than may be suitable for the language classroom. This questionnaire will allow you to negotiate a code of behavior which is more appropriate for your teaching style and the methodology of *Move Up*.

- Ask the students to read the questionnaire and answer it for themselves.

2. Aim: to practice listening for main ideas.
- 🔊 Play the tape and ask the students to put a check by the questions which the speaker answers with *Yes*. Then ask them to take notes about her answers.

3. Aim: to practice speaking.
- Ask the students to work in pairs and to compare notes with each other. Ask them to add as much detail as they can remember about what the American said.

- 🔊 Play the tape again and check this activity with the whole class.

Answers
1. Yes. "Hi, how are you doing?" or "Hi, Bill, what's up?" or "Good evening."
2. No.
3. Maria.
4. Yes. "I'm sorry I'm late."
5. The students.
6. No.
7. Yes.
8. No, not in a test.
9. During the class.
10. All of them except reference books and field trips.
11. She doesn't take any other classes.
12. Teacher tells them.
13. No.

SPEAKING AND WRITING

1. Aim: to practice speaking.
- Ask the students to talk about their answers to the questions. Are their answers very different from the American's answers? Ask them to talk about behavior in the different classrooms.

2. Aim: to practice writing.
- Ask the students to write a detailed description of what happens at the beginning, during, and at the end of a class in another subject and compare it with an American language class.

- You may like to ask the students to do this for homework.

Progress Check 1–5

GENERAL COMMENTS

You can work through this Progress Check in the order shown, or concentrate on areas which may have caused difficulty in Lessons 1 to 5. You can also let the students choose the activities they would like to, or feel the need to do.

VOCABULARY

1. **Aim: to review the vocabulary in Lessons 1 to 5 with a crossword.**
● You may want to limit the time spent on this activity to ten minutes. It will give the students a good opportunity to look very carefully at the vocabulary boxes and choose words to fit their crosswords.

2. **Aim: to focus on parts of speech.**
● The students have already done some activities to do with parts of speech in Lessons 1 to 5.

> **Answers**
> talk *n* and *v*   head *n* and *v*   drink *n* and *v*
> fly *n* and *v*   start *n* and *v*   rent *n* and *v*
> slice *n* and *v*   heat *n* and *v*

3. **Aim: to explain the purpose of the *Wordbank*.**
● It is important that the students realize that language acquisition in general, and vocabulary acquisition in particular, is only effective if they take an active part in the process. This means choosing words which are personally useful and recording them. Most students will only be able to retain about eight or nine words a lesson, so while the twenty or so words presented in the box are the most important ones to learn, the students must make the final selection. The *Wordbank* is designed to help the students organize their vocabulary records in a systematic way.

GRAMMAR

1. **Aim: to review asking questions in the present simple.**

> **Answers**
> 1. Where do you live?
> 2. Are you married?
> 3. What do you do?
> 4. When do you start work? *or*
>   What time do you start work?
> 5. When do you finish work? *or*
>   What time do you finish work?
> 6. What do you do in the evenings?
> 7. What do you do on weekends?
> 8. Where do you go on vacation?

2. **Aim: to review the position of adverbs of frequency in sentences.**
● Make sure the students make true sentences for their own countries.

3. **Aim: to review short answers when talking about likes and dislikes.**
● Make sure the students answer the questions according to their own likes and dislikes.

4. **Aim: to review the formation of present participles.**

> **Answers**
> closing, visiting, flying, wearing, making, singing, getting, throwing, crossing, going, staying, cutting

5. Aim: to review the distinction between the present simple and the present continuous.

Answers
1. Tanya **comes** from Russia.
2. She **is visiting** New York.
3. She **is taking** a vacation.
4. She **speaks** English quite well.
5. She **is staying** with friends in New York.
6. She **is enjoying** her visit.
7. She **goes** shopping most days.
8. She **says** she wants to come back soon.

6. Aim: to review the use of articles.

Answers
1. There's **a** radio in **the** living room.
2. Would you like **a** cup of – coffee?
3. They have **a** large house in **the** country.
4. We have **a** son and – two daughters.
5. **The** children are outside in **the** yard.
6. What's **the** main room in your apartment?
7. She spoke – very good French on **the** phone.
8. I flew to – Montana and spent – two weeks in **the** Rockies.

SOUNDS

1. Aim: to practice /s/, /z/, and /ɪz/.

Answers

/s/	/z/	/ɪz/
gets	does	finishes
looks	goes	refuses
smokes	leaves	
wants	sings	

2. Aim: to practice /ɪ/ and /iː/.
● 📼 Play the tape and stop after each word. Ask the students to say the words out loud.

Answers

/ɪ/	/iː/
it	eat
fifty	fifteen
live	leave
sit	seat

3. Aim: to focus on the use of intonation to show interest.
● 📼 Play the tape and stop after each sentence. Ask the students to say the sentences out loud.

Answers
1. What's your name? ✔
2. How old are you?
3. Where do you live? ✔
4. Do you live with your parents? ✔
5. Are you married?
6. Is that your brother?
7. Is that your husband? ✔
8. Do you have a sister?

SPEAKING AND WRITING

1. Aim: to present some very basic rules of punctuation in English.
● You may like to ask the students to read the rules of punctuation and simply decide if they are the same or different to the rules in their own language.

Answers
1. We don't usually visit people without an invitation.
2. When we meet people for the first time we say, "How do you do."
3. When do you use first names in your country?
4. Your friend is called Jim Smith. Do you call him Jim or Mr. Smith?
5. It's usual to use first names with people when you get to know them.

2. Aim: to practice using the present tenses and to review the vocabulary areas of customs and habits.
r● Ask the students to work in small groups and to dis-cuss these questions. The main headings refer to some of the issues discussed in Lesson 1, but the questions may be different to ones answered in that lesson. Even if you are teaching students who all come from the same cul-ture, there may be small differences in behavior and attitudes. If so, you can use this to draw attention to the possibility of more important differences with people from other cultures.

3. Aim: to practice writing.
● The students can use this opportunity to write down the main points of their discussion in 2. If there isn't time, this can be done for homework.

6

GENERAL COMMENTS

Past simple

It is expected that most students will have already come across this tense before they start *Move Up* Pre-intermediate. For this reason, both regular and irregular verbs are presented in this lesson. The two main areas of possible difficulty or error will be the mispronunciation of the past simple endings, and the use of the past simple after *did* instead of the infinitive in questions. Specific coverage of the pronunciation point is given in the *Sounds* section of this lesson, and questions are presented in Lesson 7.

Dictionaries

Using a monolingual or bilingual dictionary in class is a good way of preparing the students to take responsibility for their learning. At first you may want to do some directed activities with dictionaries, but after a while, most students use dictionaries if and when they need to. However, it is equally important to ensure that they don't overuse the dictionary and that they develop the necessary techniques for dealing with unfamiliar words. It may be necessary to impose a rule that they do not look up more than, say, six words in a passage. This will encourage the students to choose these words carefully, and not look up the words they can guess. It is also important not to treat a reading passage as an opportunity for vocabulary building. There are many words in this passage which are not essential at this level, and the words which are suitable for acquisition are included in the vocabulary box.

VOCABULARY AND READING

1. **Aim: to prepare for reading by predicting something of the background to the passage.**
   - Ask the students questions, for example, *What can you see? Where is this? How can you tell? What's the weather like?*

2. **Aim: to present the words in the box and to prepare the students for the passage.**
   - Tell the students that two of the words can only be nouns, and two can only be verbs. All of the other words can be both, often with very different meanings.

   > **Answers**
   > bridge *n, v*   build *v*   check *n, v*   cost *n, v*   cross *n, v*
   > fit *n, v*   lead *n, v*   name *n, v*   principle *n*   ship *n, v*
   > smile *n, v*   spend *v*   trip *n, v*

3. **Aim: to practice reading for main ideas.**
   - The task is designed to ensure that the students read the passage for its main idea and don't get stuck on difficult vocabulary. Explain that the passage is at a slightly higher level of difficulty than the students' present level, but that they need to be exposed to examples of authentic English in class, in order to prepare them for real-life conditions of language use.

   > **Answer**
   > The picture is of London Bridge, now in Arizona, U.S.A.

4. **Aim: to present past simple affirmative and negative statements; to practice inferring.**
   - This activity involves simple statements which encourage the students to read between the lines and infer what the writer really says. Ask them to read the passage again on their own, and then to check their answers in pairs.

   > **Answers**
   > 1. False. He's a millionaire.
   > 2. False. He built Lake Havasu City in the Arizona desert.
   > 3. False. The bridge cost $2.5 million; the whole project cost $7.5 million.
   > 4. False. He detoured the Colorado river so it flowed under the bridge.
   > 5. True.

GRAMMAR

1. Aim: to focus on regular and irregular verbs.
- Ask the students to read the information about the past simple in the grammar box.
- This activity is designed to use the verbs in the passage to introduce, or remind the students about, the difference between regular and irregular verbs.

> **Answers**
> **Regular:** finished, flowed, named, needed, started
> **Irregular:** was/were, cost, put, thought

2. Aim: to focus on the formation of regular verbs.
- This activity allows the students to look at regular past simple endings and to guess the infinitive form.

> **Answers**
> carry, close, continue, dance, decide, like, live, stop, travel, try

- The students may not be able to figure out this rule with complete accuracy, but the process of doing so will be generative enough to provide the basic principles. Suggest that they turn to the Grammar Review to check their answers.

3. Aim: to focus on irregular verbs.
- This activity allows the students to work from given information about irregular verbs to produce their infinitive forms, which they should already know.

> **Answers**
> become, come, choose, cost, cut, do, hit, have, hear, know, make, meet, put, run, read, say, shut, take, tell, understand, go, write

4. Aim: to focus on patterns in irregular verbs.
- Despite the fact that the verbs in the list are irregular, there are nevertheless some patterns which make some of them similar.

> **Answers**
> Verbs which have the same form in the present and past simple: cost, cut, hit, put, read, shut
> Verb which has the same form but sounds different: read (present simple /riːd/, past simple /red/)

SOUNDS

1. Aim: to focus on the sounds of past simple endings.
- Explain that the *-(e)d* ending may be pronounced in three ways. Write the three phonemes on the board.
- Ask them to predict which column the words go in.
- 🖭 Play the tape and pause after each word. Ask a student to write the word in the correct column on the board.

> **Answers**
> /t/: finished walked danced
> /d/: continued enjoyed called
> /ɪd/: started wanted expected

2. Aim: to practice the pronunciation of past simple endings.
- 🖭 Explain that after an unvoiced sound the ending is pronounced /t/, after a voiced sound it is /d/, and after *t* or *d* it is pronounced /ɪd/.

SPEAKING

1. Aim: to give practice in using regular and irregular past verbs; to discuss reactions to the text.
- The students may think, as did many people around the world at the time, that moving the London Bridge to Arizona at great expense was nothing more than the whim of a millionaire. However, Lake Havasu City has become one of the top tourist sites in the state of Arizona, and the tourist industry has in turn brought prosperity to a region that was formerly a desert. In addition, when Robert McCulloch bought the bridge, it was in desperate need of renovation (it was, in fact, falling down), but due to a lack of funds such work would not have been carried out. In other words, McCulloch's "whim" saved an historic monument from destruction.

2. Aim: to give practice using regular and irregular past verbs; to practice telling short anecdotes.
- Tell the students that the aim of this activity is to tell a story about an expensive purchase. Their stories do not have to be true, but should be interesting and convincing. They should try to think of as much detail as possible to support their story.
- Ask them to work in small groups, and to begin telling their story as soon as they feel ready. The others in the group will listen to the story, react to it, and then ask any clarifying questions before taking a vote on whether the story was true or not.

7

GENERAL COMMENTS

Past simple questions and short answers

Common mistakes are:

– the use of the past simple and not the infinitive after *did* in questions: *What did you saw there?*

– the inversion of the noun or pronoun and the infinitive: *What did see you there?*

– the omission of the auxiliary *did: What saw you there?*

As soon as anyone makes one of these mistakes, write the sentence on the board and cross it out. Then each time a student makes a similar error, you can point to the sentence and draw attention to the general pattern.

Level of difficulty

The passage has not been adapted for use by language students, but the tasks are suitable for pre-intermediate students. It is important to expose them to as much real-life English as possible, although it is equally important not to discourage them by giving them too much material at too high a level. In *Move Up* pre-intermediate, authentic and ungraded material are accompanied by graded tasks.

READING

1. **Aim: to prepare for reading by discussing the topic of the text; to scan the text for specific information.**

● Students need to know that traveler's checks are a form of money that are bought in your home country and exchanged for foreign currency when you travel abroad. The amount of the check (in the currency where you bought the check) is printed in several places and cannot be changed. Traveler's checks are a secure way of carrying large amounts of money because you have to sign them when you buy them, and sign them again in front of the bank teller, who will compare the signatures before giving you cash.

● Ask the students to read the passage and find out how the first traveler's check was invented.

> **Answer**
>
> J. C. Fargo, the president of American Express, had a lot of trouble with his letter of credit when he took a trip to Europe and often had problems getting money. This made him angry so he told M. F. Berry, one of his employees, to find a solution. He invented the first traveler's check.

2. **Aim: to practice reading for specific information; to prepare for the presentation of negatives and questions in the simple past.**

● You may need to deal with some vocabulary issues before proceeding. In order to help the students develop the skill of dealing with unfamiliar words, ask them to choose up to six words which you will explain.

● Ask the students to read the passage and to mark the sentences true or false according to the passage.

> **Answers**
>
> 1. False. He was an employee of the company.
> 2. True.
> 3. False. He had to wait a long time to get his money, and some banks refused to give him money at all.
> 4. True.
> 5. False. You signed the top line.
> 6. False. It was an instant success.
> 7. False. He wanted to buy a camel blanket.
> 8. True.
> 9. False. He didn't want to take cash.

GRAMMAR

1. Aim: to present past simple *yes/no* questions and short answers.

● Ask the students to read the information about the past simple in the grammar box.

● Ask one or two students
Was M. F. Berry the president of the American Express Company?
Did J. C. Fargo go to Europe in 1890?
Elicit the answers *No, he wasn't* and *Yes, he did*. You may want to do the whole exercise orally like this.

● Ask the students to work in pairs and check their answers to *Reading* activity 2. Make sure that they form the questions correctly and use short answers. Explain that only *yes/no* questions with *be* (and modals) do not use *did/didn't* in answers.

2. Aim: to practice writing *Wh*- questions.

● Make sure the students have read and understood the information in the grammar box about the use of the auxiliary in subject and object questions. Explain that they must re-read the passage carefully in order to formulate the questions. Check that they put a question mark at the end of the sentence.

> **Possible Answers**
> 1. Who was the president of the American Express Company from 1881 to 1914?
> 2. When did he go to Europe?
> 3. What did he take with him?
> 4. Why was he angry when he returned to the United States?
> 5. When did M. F. Berry invent the traveler's check?
> 6. How did you identify yourself when you cashed a traveler's check?
> 7. Where was the American tourist in the story?
> 8. What did he want to buy?

● You may want to continue this activity by writing on the board a few things which happened in the past, such as dates or important events and ask the students to write the questions. They can also write a list of dates and events themselves, and give them to other students to write questions.

VOCABULARY AND SPEAKING

1. Aim: to present the words in the vocabulary box; to develop an awareness of words which go together and to help the process of vocabulary acquisition.

● This activity involves work on verb complementation, which is an important part of vocabulary development. Students will notice that some verbs (intransitive) take no object at all, others (transitive) take a direct object, others take a direct and an indirect object, while others take a prepositional phrase. Some verbs can be followed by another verb in the infinitive, others by a gerund. They do not need to know the terminology for classifying verb complements at this point, but should realize that there *are* groups of verbs that behave in the same way.

> **Answers**
> ● nodded (—), smiled (—)
> ● found (the solution), got (his money), identified (yourself), pulled out (the cash), shook (his head), signed (your name), took (a letter of credit),
> ● gave (him the blanket), made (him furious), told (foreign banks how much money)
> ● looked (at the money), paid (for something), returned (to the United States), thought (about the problem), waited (to get his money)
> ● decided (to take), refused (to give), wanted (to buy)

2. Aim: to practice using the past simple tense; to use newly acquired vocabulary items.

● Tell the students to think of a story about something that happened to them while they were on a trip or a vacation. This activity will prepare them for the topic of Lesson 8. They have to include five of the verbs in activity 1, so they will need some time to prepare their stories.

3. Aim: to recognize newly acquired vocabulary items; to provide further speaking practice.

● Ask the students to listen to their partner's story and try to identify the five words he or she chose in activity 2. When they have checked their answers with their partner, they can ask questions about the story they heard.

8

GENERAL COMMENTS

Listening

There are several problems with using recorded material in class. Students are deprived of the visual and information clues which they would have if they were personally involved in the conversation. They are rarely confident in their listening ability because they are not in control of the speed at which the information needs to be processed and understood. They try to understand every word, and may panic if there is something difficult. The strategy for listening practice in *Move Up* is to give students the chance to hear authentic or typical spoken English and to do tasks which focus more on the general sense than on specific words. The comprehension checks in *Move Up* involve checking and crossing, numbering, lettering, or making some gesture of the pen, rather than producing language. Another major problem is simply getting the students to listen, so the preparation phase is particularly important in creating a pedagogical motivation. Finally, even if this motivation to listen is created, it has to be maintained by a task to complete while the students are listening. You may decide you want them to listen and follow the transcript at the back of the book, but this should supplement and not replace the tasks suggested. Using tapescripts generally involves focusing on every word, which is not helpful towards developing listening competence.

VOCABULARY

1. **Aim: to present the words in the vocabulary box; to prepare for the listening passages.**
- Before the students begin, write the four travel situations on the board and ask students to suggest words which go with them.

- Ask the students to match the words in the box to the four situations.

> **Possible Answers**
> **a train journey:** book, connection, delay, one way, passenger, platform, reservation, round trip, departure, fare, luggage, schedule, ticket
> **a boat journey:** cabin, delay, departure, fare, ferry, harbor, luggage, one way, passenger, reservation, round trip, schedule, terminal, ticket
> **a plane flight:** airport, boarding pass, book, business class, cabin, check in, connection, delay, departure, fare, luggage, one way, passenger, reservation, round trip, schedule, terminal, ticket, take off,
> **hotel accommodation:** bed and breakfast, book, check in, check out, double room, lift, luggage, reservation, single room

2. **Aim: to expand vocabulary connected with travel situations; to help the students organize their vocabulary learning.**
- Ask the students to add the words they suggested at the start of activity 1 to their lists.

LISTENING AND SPEAKING

1. **Aim: to prepare the students to listen to the passage.**
- Ask the students to look at the phrases taken from the story and to predict the travel situation.

> **Answer**
> Hotel accommodation.

- Ask the students to think about the vocabulary they are likely to hear.

2. **Aim: to practice listening to a passage of continuous English.**
- 🔊 Play the tape and ask if they guessed correctly in activity 1.

3. **Aim: to check the students have understood the main ideas.**
- Ask the students to work in pairs and to number the events in the order they heard them.

> **Answers**
> | | |
> |---|---|
> | sat down on the tiny single bed | [6] |
> | knocked on the door | [2] |
> | slept in the car that night | [10] |
> | didn't have a reservation | [1] |
> | wanted to check out | [7] |
> | asked if he had a room | [3] |
> | left my suitcase in my car | [9] |
> | picked up a key from behind the desk | [4] |
> | was frightened by the man in the office | [8] |
> | showed me a very dusty room | [5] |

- 🔊 Play the tape again. The students may like to follow the tapescript as they listen.

4. **Aim: to practice using the past simple.**
- Ask if anyone has been in a situation where something went wrong. It doesn't have to be a travel situation. Ask them to tell the rest of the class about it.

GRAMMAR

1. **Aim: to practice using the past simple and expressions of past time.**
- Ask the students to think about important or memorable events in their lives.

2. **Aim: to practice using the past simple and expressions of past time.**
- Ask the students to work in pairs and to show each other their expressions of past time. They should ask and answer questions about what happened. Go around and check that everyone is using the past simple correctly.

3. **Aim: to focus on *because*.**
- Ask the students to read the information about *so* and *because* in the grammar box.
- Ask them to join the two parts of the sentences. There's no need to write the full sentences.

> **Answers**
> 1. d 2. b 3. a 4. c

4. **Aim: to focus on *so*.**
- The students will have to write the sentences in full.

> **Answers**
> 1. He didn't expect to stay there long so he didn't have a hotel reservation.
> 2. There were no lights on so he walked past the motel.
> 3. The room was dirty and unpleasant so he decided to leave.
> 4. He was so scared so he locked himself in his car.

WRITING

1. **Aim: to practice writing a story.**
- Ask the students to form groups of five or six and if possible to sit in a circle. Then ask them to write an opening sentence of their own on a separate piece of paper (i.e. not fixed in a notebook).

2. **Aim: to practice writing a story.**
- Ask them to pass the piece of paper with their sentence to the person on their right, and receive a sentence from the person on the left. They continue the story from the point left off by the sentence on the new piece of paper and not the story they began writing in 1.
- They continue writing sentences and passing the paper on until the story is finished. They then all have a piece of paper with sentences written by other people.

3. **Aim: to rewrite the story using *and, but, so*, and *because*.**
- Ask them to rewrite the story using *and, but, so*, and *because*.
- Ask the students to read each other's stories.

4. **Aim: to give further writing practice.**
- If there isn't time, you can ask the students to do this for homework.

9

GENERAL COMMENTS

Possessive adjectives

Most students will already have come across possessive adjectives in a previous course, so this lesson will be review for them. The main difficulty for speakers of languages in which nouns have a gender is that the possessive adjective refers to the person or thing it replaces rather than to the noun that follows. For example, *Steve's wife = his wife* not *her wife, Caroline's husband = her husband* not *his husband*. Another common error, even among native speakers is to write *it's* for the possessive adjective. This is, in fact, the contracted form of *it is*.

Possessive 's

This is also known as the *Saxon genitive*. The exact position of the apostrophe depends on whether the noun is singular or plural, regular or irregular. Once again, it is common even among native speakers to place the apostrophe in the wrong position. Among purists, the seriousness of the error is compounded by the simplicity of this rule. Singular names ending in *-s* usually have *'s*, e.g. *Charles's sons, James's house*, but there are exceptions. You don't use an article when the first word is a proper name, e.g. *Larry's wife* not *the Larry's wife*. We often use the genitive *'s* with stores and professions, e.g. *the dry cleaner's, the dentist's*. Sometimes the genitive is dropped when the noun can operate as an adjective, e.g. *the car door, the table leg*, but this is more advanced than can usefully be dealt with at this level.

VOCABULARY AND LISTENING

1. Aim: to present the words in the box and to pre-teach new vocabulary in the listening passage.
- Write *aunt-uncle, boy-girl* on the board. Then ask the students to pair the other words. It's probably best to do this activity orally with the whole class.

> **Answers**
> **Pairs:** aunt-uncle, boy-girl, boyfriend-girlfriend, brother-sister, child-parent, daughter-son, father-mother, grandfather-grandmother, husband-wife, man-woman, nephew-niece
> **No pairs:** friend, cousin

- You may need to point out that the child-parent pair is the only one not based on gender. Ask the students to write down the words in their vocabulary books.

2. Aim: to practice listening for specific information.
- Explain that the students are going to listen to an American woman, Kathy, talking about her family. Some of the members of her family are in the photo. Ask the students to predict which words she is likely to use.

- 📼 Play the tape and ask the students to draw a line to show the relationship between Kathy and the people she mentions.

> **Answers**
> Pat–grandmother   Tony–uncle
> Ray–brother   Larry–husband
> Kelly–sister   Carol–mother
> Christine–aunt   Craig–father

GRAMMAR

1. Aim: to focus on the possessive 's.
- Ask the students to read the information about possessive adjectives and the possessive *'s* in the grammar box.

- Ask them to work in pairs and to do the exercise.

> **Answers**
> 1. Kathy is Ray's sister.
> 2. Ray is Kelly's brother.
> 3. Kelly is Craig's daughter.
> 4. Craig is Carol's husband.
> 5. Carol is Kathy's mother.
> 6. Kathy is Larry's wife.

2. Aim: to focus on the possessive adjectives.
- Go around and point to objects which belong to people, e.g. *Mario's book, Hitomi's pen*. Then say *his book, her pen*.

- Ask the students to do the exercise.

> **Answers**
> 1. Kathy is his sister.
> 2. Ray is her brother.
> 3. Kelly is his daughter.
> 4. Craig is her husband.
> 5. Carol is her mother.
> 6. Kathy is his wife.

SOUNDS

1. **Aim: to focus on the /ə/ sound.**

● The /ə/ sound or *schwa* is one of the most common sounds in English. It represents an unstressed syllable. The large number of unstressed syllables in English is what gives the impression that English is spoken rather quickly or gabbled.

● ▭ Play the tape and ask the students to underline the /ə/.

> **Answers**
> together parent suppose opinion advice
> husband woman

● Ask the students to say the words out loud.

2. **Aim: to focus on contrastive stress.**

● Remind the students that the words the speakers consider to be important are the words they stress. In this activity, wrong information is corrected and stressed, to underline the contrast between the correct and wrong information.

● ▭ Play the tape and ask a student to correct the information, changing the stressed word each time. You may need to stop the tape at each pause.

> **Answers**
> 1. No, Larry is Kathy's **husband**.
> 2. No, **Larry** is Kathy's husband.
> 3. No, **Kathy's** husband.
> 4. No, Larry is Kathy's **husband**.
> 5. No, Larry is **Kathy's** husband.
> 6. No, **Larry** is Kathy's husband.

● ▭ Play the tape again and ask the class to do the activity together.

READING AND SPEAKING

1. **Aim: to practice reading for main ideas.**

● The activity is designed to encourage the students not to get distracted with unfamiliar vocabulary. Try to resist answering vocabulary questions at this stage. Ask the students to match the questions with each paragraph.

> **Answers**
> a. paragraph 2
> b. paragraph 1
> d. paragraph 4
> e. paragraph 3
> The extra question is c.

● You may want to answer a few questions about vocabulary now. Try to limit it to six or seven words in total.

2. **Aim: to practice separating general from specific information.**

● It is important to be able to see when a writer is making a generalization and when he or she is making a specific point. Ask the students to re-read the passage and to find out which paragraphs contain generalizations and which contain specific information.

> **Answers**
> **Specific information:** paragraphs 1, 2, and 4
> **Some general information:** paragraphs 3 and 4

3. **Aim: to talk about reactions to the passage.**

● In many cultures, it is acceptable to talk about your family to people you don't know very well. If this is the case with your students, ask them to answer the questions in activity 1 and talk about their families. If your students come from a culture where it is less acceptable to talk about personal matters, ask them to work in groups of three or four to answer the questions in a very general way.

● Ask the students to report back to the rest of the class and tell each other about family life in their country or countries. It doesn't matter if your students all come from the same cultural background. There may still be varying reactions that will make the students more sensitive to cultural differences.

10

GENERAL COMMENTS

Have (got); There is

These structures are probably not new to the students but may still be causing some trouble, especially in the negative and question forms. *Have (got)* is a common source of problems for students, since the auxiliary verb is different depending on whether *got* is used or not. Unfortunately, both forms are very common in American English, so students simply have to learn how to manipulate the two forms. Much of the time, however, they can use *have* as the main verb (and *do* as the auxiliary) without sounding unnatural.

Vocabulary

The vocabulary area covered in this lesson, town facilities and related adjectives, is a very large one. It may be advisable to restrict active acquisition to items which are personally relevant to the student and the town where he or she lives.

VOCABULARY AND LISTENING

1. Aim: to present the words in the vocabulary box and to pre-teach important items to be heard in the listening passage.

● Before the students begin this activity, write the title of the lesson on the board, and ask them to suggest any words they are likely to see in the lesson.

● Ask the students to look at the words in the box and check the ones which they can use to describe their town. These are the words which they should make an effort to learn. They should also list other words which they have come across which can be used to describe their town. Some of the vocabulary in Lessons 4 and 5 will be useful, so suggest that they should look again at the relevant vocabulary boxes and notes to see which ones they can add to their lists.

2. Aim: to practice listening for specific information.

● 🔲 Explain that the students will hear some of the words in the box, and that they should check them as they hear them.

Tapescript and Answers

INTERVIEWER What's it like living in Taipei?

LAURA Oh, I love it! The people are so friendly and helpful, and it's big, but not too big, you know?

INTERVIEWER What's the population?

LAURA About three and a half million, I think… I'm not sure. But it doesn't feel really congested, like a lot of other big cities. It's fairly polluted, I guess… nothing like L.A., though! And it's got everything… **parks**, **museums**… fantastic museums!… **restaurants** to die for…

INTERVIEWER Is it very industrialized?

LAURA Oh, sure… out in the suburbs there are, you know, the **factories** and the industrial estates, and… uh… the city center is pretty modern. But there is still a lot of the "old" Taipei… like Wanhua, which has houses and shops and **temples** and family **shrines** that are all about 100 years old. I go down there a lot to take photos and just watch people.

INTERVIEWER What are the people like?

LAURA Oh, really friendly and helpful… I'm taking Chinese classes at the **university** now, but when I first arrived I was totally lost, and people kept helping me out… taking me places, and translating for me.

INTERVIEWER Wow! Uh… Is Taipei expensive?

LAURA Well, it's getting that way, but I guess I get paid pretty well, so it doesn't seem… I mean, clothes and food are really cheap. But I pay about twice as much rent as I would in the United States, and my apartment is, well, teeny!

3. Aim: to check comprehension; to infer information.

● Ask the students to think about what they heard and to try to remember at least three things that Laura likes about living in Taipei. Write their ideas on the board.

● 🔲 When they are ready, play the tape again and ask a student to check off the ideas on the board as he or she hears them.

Answers

the people are so friendly and helpful; it's big, but not too big; it doesn't feel really congested; it's got everything… parks, museums, restaurants; the "old" Taipei… like Wanhua; clothes and food are really cheap

4. Aim: to present the words in the vocabulary box; to distinguish between parts of speech.

● Ask the students to underline the adjectives in the box.

Answers

bad, beautiful, boring, busy, cheap, cold, crowded, dangerous, dirty, excellent, expensive, good, interesting, large, medium-sized, modern, old, safe, small

● Ask the students to suggest words to describe aspects of their town and write them on the board.

● Ask the students to suggest adjectives which can go with the aspects of their town. Write the adjectives on the board under the aspects.

5. Aim: to practise listening for main ideas.

- 🔲 Explain to the students that they are going to listen to six people talking about different aspects of their town. The students should listen for the main idea and not worry about difficult vocabulary.

> **Answers**
> 1. cost of living
> 2. traffic
> 3. architecture
> 4. size
> 5. climate
> 6. safety

- You may want to play the tape again when you have checked the answers.

GRAMMAR

1. Aim: to focus on the use of contractions.

- Ask the students to read the information in the grammar box.

- Ask the students to do the activity orally.

- Ask the students to write the sentences in which contractions are possible.

> **Answers**
> 1. The university has a park. (No change)
> 2. There's a modern subway system.
> 3. He's got a swimming pool.
> 4. I've got tickets to the theater.
> 5. Taipei has some beautiful temples. (No change)
> 6. There's a great view from this window.

2. Aim: to practice using the target structures.

- Ask the students to describe their hometown or the town where they live. You can ask them questions using the words in *Vocabulary and Listening* activity 1 to help them, e.g. *Does it have an art gallery? Is there a beach? Are there any good restaurants?* and elicit *Yes/No* answers.

- Ask the students to talk about their towns in pairs. Go around and make sure they are using the structures correctly.

WRITING

1. Aim: to read and infer advantages and disadvantages.

- Ask the students to make a list of the advantages and disadvantages which Laura mentions.

> **Answers**
> **Advantages:** interesting, people are polite and friendly, not crowded or stressful, streets are clean, parks are well-kept, a lot of beautiful temples and shrines, beautiful old parts, food and clothes are cheap
> **Disadvantages:** air is quite polluted, too many tourists, malls, fast-food places, video games, apartments are expensive, prices in some stores are high

- You may like to ask the students whether they agree with what Laura considers to be advantages and disadvantages. For example, some people may think that malls, fast-food places, and video games are not disadvantages!

2. Aim: to link two parts of a sentence with *and* and *but*.

- All of the advantages can be linked together using *and*. Ask the students to join two advantages or two disadvantages with *and*.

- Not all of the advantages and disadvantages can be linked using *but*, so make sure that the students choose the pairs carefully.

3. Aim: to write notes about the advantages and disadvantages of towns.

- If the students all come from the same city, you can do this orally with the whole class. Ask the students to suggest advantages and disadvantages and write them on the board. They can include aspects which have not been mentioned so far.

4. Aim: to write linked sentences about the advantages and disadvantages of towns.

- Ask the students to join together the notes they made in activity 3 with *and* and *but*, and write full sentences.

5. Aim: to write a short description of a town.

- Ask the students to use the sentences they wrote in activity 4 in a short description of their town. The reading passage about Taipei can be used as a model. Suggest that they include some more personalized information in their descriptions.

- This activity can be done for homework.

Fluency 2

GENERAL COMMENTS

Attitudes towards time differ from culture to culture. Some cultures are very conscious of the time, and punctual arrival for appointments is very important. Other cultures see time as a much more flexible concept, and make sure that they aren't bullied by agreed meeting times. You may like to introduce your learners to the concept of *clock time* and *appropriate time*. Clock time can best be illustrated by this example: *It's one o'clock. I must have lunch.* Appropriate time is illustrated: *I'm hungry, I must have something to eat.* Point out that most business communities will be oriented towards clock time, and more conservative, traditional cultures will be oriented to appropriate time. You may like to ask the students if they think they belong to a culture which is more clock time or appropriate time.

LISTENING AND SPEAKING

1. Aim: to prepare for listening; to practice dealing with difficult words.
- Remind students that they don't always have to understand what every word means when they read or listen to English. In this activity they can't even see what every word is. The activity will help them practice guessing the meaning of difficult words.

- Ask the students to check their answers in pairs.

2. Aim: to listen for specific information.
- 📼 Play the tape and ask the students to check their answers to 1.

> **Answers**
> 1. like; on; start; leave; Six; later
> 2. time; leave; now; long; take; About; away; miss

3. Aim: to practice speaking.
- Check that everyone has completed their conversations with the correct words.

- Ask the students to work in pairs and to act out the conversations.

4. Aim: to practice speaking.
- Ask the students to use the conversations in 1 as models for new conversations in the situations described. They should prepare the conversations paying attention to different times.

- When they are ready, ask the students to act out the conversations they have prepared.

5. Aim: to practice reading and reacting to statements; to prepare for listening.
- The statements all focus on time and the times people do things. They are naturally in the present simple tense as they describe routines and habits.
- Ask the students to talk about their answers to the statements in pairs. You may like to go through this with the whole class.

6. Aim: to practice listening for main ideas.
- 📼 The students will have prepared themselves for the listening passage in activity 5. Play the tape and ask the students to decide which statements are true for the United States.

> **Answers**
> Most people get up at about seven o'clock in the morning. ✔
> People generally start work at nine o'clock. ✔
> There's usually a coffee break at eleven o'clock.
> You have to be on time for appointments. ✔
> You can arrive late for meetings with friends. ✔
> Lunch is usually at noon.
> It's common to spend time with co-workers after work.
> People don't usually work late.
> Dinner is usually at eight o'clock.
> Most people are in bed before midnight. ✔

7. Aim: to practice speaking; to provide an opportunity for a second listening.
- Ask the students to try and reconstitute in detail what Bill said. You may like to ask the students to check what they've remembered with other pairs in the class.

- 📼 Play the tape again and ask students to check their answers.

FUNCTIONS

1. Aim: to focus on ways of telling the time.

● Ask the students to read the information in the functions box. Students will have already come across this language at earlier stages in their English classes, so use this opportunity to check that they can still manipulate this language successfully. You may like to do these activities orally with the whole group.

● Ask the students to write the times in clock form.

Answers

 One o'clock.

 Ten after two/Two ten.

 Ten to three/Two fifty.

 Five (minutes) after three/ Three oh five.

 A quarter after four/Four fifteen.

 Twenty after five/Five twenty.

 Half past six/Six thirty.

 Twenty five to seven/Six thirty-five.

 Twenty to eight/Seven forty.

 A quarter to nine/Eight forty-five.

 Five to eleven/Ten fifty-five.

 Twelve o'clock noon/Midnight.

 It's nearly ten thirty.

 It's exactly seven fifteen.

 It's just after six.

 It's about five thirty.

2. Aim: to practice telling the time.

● Ask the students to say what times the clocks show. They can check their answers in pairs.

Answers

It's eleven o'clock/It's nearly eleven.
It's just after two.
It's twenty-five to two/one thirty-five.
It's twenty five to six/five thirty-five.
It's twenty after seven/seven twenty.
It's half past eight/eight thirty.

3. Aim: to practice listening for main ideas.

● Remind the students that establishing the context of a conversation or some other listening passage is a useful way of revealing the meaning of a new word.

● 🔲 Play the tape and ask the students to listen and guess what the situation is for each dialogue.

Answers

Dialogue 1: at an airport
Dialogue 2: at a family breakfast
Dialogue 3: a recorded phone message
Dialogue 4: at a train station

4. Aim: to practice using the language for telling the time.

● Ask the students to remember the times they heard in the dialogues.

● 🔲 Play the tape again and ask the students to check their answers.

Answers

Dialogue 1: Ten thirty
Dialogue 2: Ten after eight
Dialogue 3: Eight thirty
Dialogue 4: Nine fifteen

READING AND WRITING

1. Aim: to practice reading for main ideas; to practice comparing cultures.

● Ask the students to read the comments and to look for any which they might expect to hear in their own country. Do the comments show examples of *clock time* or *appropriate time*?

2. Aim: to practice writing; to practice comparing cultures.

● Ask the students to write sentences about the attitudes toward time that each statement reveals.

● You may like to ask the students to do this activity for homework.

Progress Check 6–10

GENERAL COMMENTS

You can work through this Progress Check in the order shown, or concentrate on areas which may have caused difficulty in Lessons 6 to 10. You can also let the students choose the activities which they would like to, or feel the need to do.

VOCABULARY

1. **Aim: to review vocabulary and to remember words which can be grouped together.**
● This activity is not meant to be a serious word-association test, so give the students between five to ten seconds to think of a suitable word. Play one round of the game with the class as a whole.

● Ask the students to work in pairs and continue playing the game.

2. **Aim: to focus on compound nouns.**
● In some languages it is not possible to combine two nouns to make a compound noun. In English the first noun operates like an adjective, but the compound usually represents a single concept. The rules for writing them as one, two, or hyphenated words are complex, so suggest to the students that they have to take note of this information at the same time as they learn the new compound noun.

Answers
round trip, hotel reservation, first class, boarding pass, airport, suitcase, credit card

3. **Aim: to help the students organize their vocabulary learning.**
● Categorizing is a useful way of organizing new vocabulary and making the learning process more effective. It is often even more effective if the students choose these categories themselves. In *Move Up* there are often categories which are suggested in the activity and then categories which the students are invited to create for themselves. This activity will give the students an opportunity to go back over Lessons 6 to 10, to remind themselves of the words presented in the vocabulary boxes, and to create new categories which consolidate the process of acquisition.

GRAMMAR

1. **Aim: to review the past simple of regular verbs.**

Answers
asked, carried, changed, continued, decided, enjoyed, finished, happened, liked, listened, lived, looked, opened, played, started, stayed, stopped, talked, tested, tried, traveled, visited, walked, watched

2. **Aim: to review the past simple of irregular verbs.**

Answers
was/were, became, did, went, got, had, knew, left, made, put, ran, saw, sat, slept, took, told

3. **Aim: to review the use of auxiliaries in questions and short answers.**

Answers
1. **Did** you enjoy your vacation? Yes, I **did**.
2. **Was** the weather good? Yes, it **was**.
3. **Did** you go to the local museums? Yes, we **did**. They **were** very interesting.
4. **Did** you send any postcards? No, we **didn't**.
5. **Did** you buy anything? No, we **didn't** have any money.
6. **Were** you happy with the hotel? Yes, we **were**.

4. **Aim: to recognize errors in past simple use.**

Answers
1. Last winter I **bought** a new coat.
2. What did M. F. Berry **invent?**
3. Why **was** J. C. Fargo angry?
4. Who **told** you about the concert? (Or: who **did** you **tell...?**)
5. Most people **didn't believe** that the London Bridge was in Arizona.
6. Why **did** he **decide** to go to the motel?

5. **Aim: to practice using *so* and *because*.**

Answers
1. I was very tired, **so** I went to bed.
2. He went to the motel **because** the hotel was full.
3. She lived with her parents **because** she couldn't afford to move out.
4. I wanted to learn English, **so** I joined this class.
5. They went home **because** you weren't here.
6. The teacher was late **because** her car broke down.

6. Aim: to practice possessive pronouns.

> **Answers**
> 1. I know **her** face. Is she famous?
> 2. We know them pretty well. **Their** children go to the same school as ours.
> 3. Phil, this is **my** friend, Mary.
> 4. What do you do, Pete? What's **your** job?
> 5. I'll call you later. What's **your** telephone number?
> 6. That belongs to me. It's got **my** name on it.

SOUNDS

1. Aim: to practice /ð/ and /θ/.

> **Answers**
> /ð /: this they
> /θ/: theater cathedral think thank you

2. Aim: to practice /ɒ/ and /əʊ/.

> **Answers**
> /ɒ/: not lots shop opera
> /əʊ/: know boat photo video don't go disco

3. Aim: to focus on friendly intonation.

> **Answers**
> 1. Did you arrive late this morning? No, I didn't. ✔
> 2. She didn't say hello. Yes, she did.
> 3. Did you give me your passport? Yes, I did. ✔
> 4. Did they pay you for the tickets?
>   No, they didn't.

WRITING

1. Aim: to practice writing a story and to create a reading comprehension check.

● This activity is designed to show the students that they can predict a great deal about a passage by looking at the questions. Make quite sure they write full answers to the questions.

● You may like to do this orally and write the sentences on the board. Every time someone guesses information, ask them *Are you sure?* If they aren't sure, then simply leave a blank.

2. Aim: to practice reading for specific information.

● The sentences the students have written in activity 1 constitute the reading passage with blanks. They have in fact written their own reading comprehension check. Ask them to read and fill in the blanks in their versions.

SPEAKING

1. Aim: to practice speaking using the past simple.

● Ask one or two students the following questions:
Did you leave home early this morning?
Did you have a vacation three months ago?
If they say *yes,* write their names on the board.

● Ask the students to go around the class with a pen and paper, asking and answering the questions, and writing down the names of people who answer *yes.* Give them about four or five minutes to do this activity.

2. Aim: to practice talking about families.

● To illustrate the expression *family tree,* draw your family tree on the board.

● Encourage the students to be as inventive or imaginative as they like about their false relatives. They can invent as much information about them as they like.

3. Aim: to practice talking about families.

● Ask the students to show other people their family trees and to talk about their families. Explain that they must guess who the false relatives are.

● Ask the class to report back on the most unlikely false relatives they found.

● If there isn't time, ask them to write a short description of their family and false relatives. They can bring the descriptions to the next class and put them on the wall for the others to read at their leisure.

11

GENERAL COMMENTS

Verb patterns (2): *to* + infinitive

In Lesson 4 the first verb pattern was presented. It was explained that when there are two verbs in a sequence the second verb is either an infinitive or an *-ing* form. This lessons focuses on *to* + infinitive.

Going to for intentions, *would like to* for ambitions

A common use of *to* + infinitive is to talk about plans, ambitions, hopes, and preferences. This is the first of a series of lessons which presents ways of talking about the future.

Questionnaires

In American magazines, questionnaires are very common. Unlike other kinds of reading material, they address the reader directly and establish a form of interaction. This is the intention of many of the passages, especially the questionnaires, in *Move Up*. The questionnaire in this lesson is not meant to be taken too seriously.

READING

1. **Aim: to prepare for reading *How Ambitious Are You?*; to create the framework for practicing the structures in the lesson.**

   ● Ask the students *Are you ambitious?* If they answer *yes*, ask them to describe what being ambitious means. Ask them if they have had the chance to achieve any of their ambitions yet.

   ● Ask the students to look at the ambitions in the list and to check the ones they have. Strictly speaking, they do not yet have the language to talk about their ambitions and say *I'd like to...*, but they can at least say which ones they checked. In *Grammar* activity 2, they will return to these ambitions.

2. **Aim: to read and answer a questionnaire.**

   ● The questions in the questionnaire demand a detailed understanding in order to be answered properly. Ask the students to write down the letter corresponding to their answers. Explain, if necessary, that the questionnaire is meant to be lighthearted.

3. **Aim: to evaluate the students' answers to the questionnaire.**

   ● Ask the students to turn to the Communication Activity on page 58 and find out how ambitious they are. Ask them if they agree with the analysis.

   ● The students may like to share their reactions with other people. Ask them to find out how other people answered each question.

   ● Finish the activity by finding out how the class as a whole answered the questionnaire.

GRAMMAR

1. Aim: to focus on the difference between *would like to* and *going to*.

● Ask the students to read the information about verb patterns in the grammar box.

● Ask the students to do the activity on their own.

● Check the answers to the activity orally.

> **Answers**
> 1. He got accepted to Harvard University. He **is going to** study there.
> 2. She has her plane ticket and **she's going to** go to Canada.
> 3. **He'd like to** buy a new car, but it's too expensive.
> 4. **I'd like to** work in television, but there aren't many jobs.
> 5. She enjoys her job. **She isn't going to** change it.
> 6. He's got a new job with a foreign company. **He is going to** work abroad.

2. Aim: to practice using *would like to* and *going to*.

● Ask the students to look back at the ambitions they checked in *Reading* activity 1. Ask one or two people to say what they'd like to do.

● Ask the students to work in pairs and to talk about their ambitions.

● Invite the students to discuss at this stage if they have any other more personal ambitions. Which do they think is the most extraordinary ambition?

VOCABULARY AND WRITING

1. Aim: to present the words in the vocabulary box; to focus on words which go together.

● The verbs in the box collocate with the nouns. Ask the students to put the verbs and the nouns together.

> **Answers**
> live abroad, earn money, study a foreign language, learn a foreign language, run a marathon, write a novel

2. Aim: to read a passage to be used as a model for guided writing practice.

● The passage is presented as a model for guided writing practice. The students will use the passage as a model when they reach activity 6. The four prompts can also be used to guide the students in the writing of their own passages.

> **Answers**
> **what she'd like to do:** learn to fly a light airplane
> **why she'd like to do it:** to know what it feels like to be in control
> **what she needs to do to achieve it:** take flying lessons
> **what she's going to do:** take her pilot's test

3. Aim: to expand notes about ambitions.

● Ask the students to make notes about why they'd like to achieve one of their ambitions.

4. Aim: to expand notes about ambitions.

● Ask the students to expand their notes by saying what they need to do to achieve this ambition.

5. Aim: to expand notes about ambitions.

● Ask the students to make notes about what they're going to do to achieve their ambition. They can be as inventive as they wish at this stage!

6. Aim: to turn notes into a paragraph using *because* and *so*.

● Remind the students that they used *so* and *because* in Lesson 8. Check that they can still use these link words correctly by asking for a few notes from one or two students and write them on the board. Then rewrite them using the link words.

12

GENERAL COMMENTS

Will

This lessons focuses on the use of *will* to make predictions or express an opinion about the future. The contraction *'ll* is used in everyday speech for *will*.

English in the future

The theme of this lesson has been chosen to stimulate some discussion about the role and uses of English as a medium of international communication. Some students, particularly those still in secondary education, may simply see English as another school subject to pass a test in, and may not realize its potential use beyond the classroom. Making students aware of how much English there is around them, even in towns away from international centers or tourist attractions, is an important student training and language awareness objective.

VOCABULARY AND SOUNDS

1. Aim: to present the words in the vocabulary box and to pre-teach any items which may occur in the listening passage.

● Write the two headings: *jobs* and *subjects* on the board and ask one or two students to put the words under the headings. Say the word *accountant* and elicit the reply *job*. Do several words like this.

● Ask the students to write the words under the two headings.

Answers

jobs	subjects
accountant	arithmetic
actor	biology
banker	chemistry
dancer	economics
doctor	history
engineer	languages
journalist	physics
politician	
secretary	

2. Aim: to focus on word stress.

● Copy the columns on the board and number them 1, 2, and 3. Point out that the numbers 1, 2, and 3 refer to the syllable that is stressed in the words which go in the columns. Say one or two of the words and ask *First, second, or third syllable?* Elicit the right answer and write the word in the correct column.

● Ask the students to list the words according to their stressed syllable.

Answers

First	Second	Third
actor	accountant	economics
banker	arithmetic	engineer
chemistry	biology	politician
dancer		
doctor		
history		
journalist		
languages		
physics		
secretary		

● 🔲 Play the tape and allow the students to check their answers.

3. Aim: to focus on /e/ and /eɪ/.

● 🔲 Ask the students to listen and repeat the words. Play the tape. Pause after each word. Make sure they distinguish between /e/ and /eɪ/.

Answers

/e/: lesson chemistry economics education secretary friend

/eɪ/: age railroad station vacation

● It is important to draw the students' attention to the different spellings represented by /eɪ/.

4. Aim: to practice using the words in the vocabulary box and to start thinking about the theme of the listening material.

● The students may not know which jobs they might need English for, and this will vary from country to country, so no answer is given. In general, however, English is often needed for the following jobs: banker, doctor, journalist, politician, and secretary. The subjects you often need to study English for are computer science, economics, and perhaps science in general.

LISTENING

1. Aim: to prepare for listening.
● This activity is designed to encourage the students to prepare their opinions on the role of English. It is also intended to let them prepare for the listening passage. Read one or two of the opinions and ask students if they agree or disagree with them.

● Then ask them to put a check or a cross by all the other predictions in the chart.

2. Aim: to practice listening for main ideas.
● 🔲 This listening passage makes no particular concessions to the non-native speaker, and especially not the student at pre-intermediate level. It is not expected that the students will understand every word, but it is hoped that they will understand enough of the general sense to be able to complete the task. Play the tape and ask the students to put a check if the speaker agrees and a cross if the speaker disagrees with the statements, and to put a question mark if it's not clear.

Answers	Maggie	Greg
Children will learn English from the age of six.	✔	✔
There will be few adults who don't speak English.	✔	✔
All classes at school will be in English.	✔	✘
Everyone will need to learn about North American culture.	✘	✔
Everyone will need English for their job.	✔	✘
Everyone will learn English at home through television and computers.	✘	✔
It will be more important to speak English than your own language.	✘	✘

3. Aim: to discuss the main ideas and details about what the speakers said.
● Ask the students to work in pairs and discuss what Maggie and Greg said. You could ask them to fill in the chart with as much detail as they can remember.

● Ask one student from each pair to go around to other pairs and find out more details. Ask them to take this information back to their partner and add it to their charts.

● 🔲 Play the tape a second time and ask the students to check their answers.

GRAMMAR

1. Aim: to practice using *I will* and *I won't* for predictions.
● Ask the students to read the information about *will* in the grammar box. Then ask them to do the exercise.

● This activity is designed to make students think about how much progress they have made and are likely to make in English by the end of the course. You may like to do the activity orally and to discuss the answers with the rest of the class.

2. Aim: to practice asking questions with *Do you think + will?*
● Ask the students to write full questions with the prompts.

> **Answers**
> 1. Do you think computers will replace secretaries and accountants?
> 2. Do you think journalists will disappear because there won't be any newspapers.
> 3. Do you think economics will be the most important school subject?
> 4. Do you think teaching by television will be very common?

3. Aim: to practice asking and answering questions about the future.
● Ask the students to work in pairs and to ask and answer the questions they wrote in activity 2.

● Ask the students to go around the class asking and answering the questions they wrote in activity 2. Ask them to put a check by the questions which people answer with *yes* and a cross by the questions people answer with *no*. They should finish the activity with a number of checks and crosses by each question.

● Find out how many people answered each question with *yes* or *no*. If there is time, ask the students to write a brief paragraph describing the results.

SPEAKING

1. Aim: to practice using *will.*
● Ask the students to check their answers to *Listening* activity 2, and to complete the chart. Ask them to make other predictions about English in the future.

2. Aim: to practice using *will.*
● Ask the students to go around asking and answering questions about the future of English based on the predictions they made in activity 1. As they go around, they should put a check or a cross by the statements.

13

GENERAL COMMENTS

Going to and *will*

It is sometimes difficult for students to understand the difference between *going to* and *will*. In *Move Up* Pre-intermediate they have come across *going to* in Lesson 11 and *will* in Lesson 12, but this lesson may be the first occasion they have come across the two structures together. After they have studied the explanation in the grammar box, it may be necessary to give further practice in the distinction between the two structures using material from the Grammar Review at the back of *Move Up* Student's Book, the Practice Book, or the Resource Pack. Reassure any student who finds the distinction difficult to absorb that it will become clearer with practice. It is a subtle distinction but the structures are very common, even at this level, and need to be acquired relatively early in the course.

Photo: The Sugar Loaf mountain in Rio de Janeiro, Brazil.

LISTENING

1. **Aim: to prepare for listening and to show how the names of certain countries and places are pronounced in English.**
   ● It is to be hoped that most students by now know how the name of their own country is pronounced in English, but they may not be acquainted with the English pronunciation of many other countries. It is not possible to do the listening activity without being able to recognize the names of the countries and places in the box, so write the following countries on the board *Brazil, Chile, Peru,* and say the places in the box and the countries out loud. Then ask if anyone knows which country the places are in.

   Answers
   Brazil: The Amazon, Rio
   Chile: Santiago, Valparaiso
   Peru: Lima, Machu Picchu

2. **Aim: to practice listening for main ideas.**
   ● 📼 The main idea to be identified is the route Ryan is planning to take. Ask the students to listen and number the places in activity 1 in the order in which Ryan mentions them.

Answers
[1]	Rio	[4]	Lima
[2]	Santiago	[5]	Machu Picchu
[3]	Valparaiso	[6]	The Amazon

3. **Aim: to listen for specific information.**
   ● The specific information in this activity is what he is planning to do. Strictly speaking, the students do not yet have the structures necessary for saying what he's *going to* do, but they should be able to talk about what he *plans* to do. Ask them to try to remember what they heard in the conversation.

   ● 📼 Play the tape again and ask the students to put the number of the place by what Ryan is going to do there.

Answers
lie on the beach	[3]
visit the ruins	[5]
do some sightseeing	[2]
spend a week in the jungle	[6]
take the cable car up the mountain	[1]
meet his girlfriend	[4]

4. **Aim: to present the difference between *going to* and *will*.**
   ● 📼 In this activity the students listen and observe the verbs Ryan uses for decisions made before the moment of speaking (*going to*) and decisions made at the moment of speaking (*will*). Explain that the tapescript is a continuation of the dialogue the students have been listening to.

Answers
CATHY Do you have a good guide book?
RYAN No, I don't, but **I'm going to get** one. It's on my list of things to buy before I go.
CATHY Well, they say the best one is "South American Handbook."
RYAN Really? Well, **I'll get** it when I go downtown.
CATHY Look, **I'm going** downtown right now because I need to do some shopping. **I'll buy** it for you at the bookstore, if you want.
RYAN Really?
CATHY Yeah, sure.
RYAN Well, **I'll give** you the money for it right now.
CATHY OK, and **I'll bring** it to your place tonight. Who knows, maybe **I'll borrow** it from you someday.
RYAN OK. Thanks a lot.

● You may like to point out that one use of *will* is to make an offer.

GRAMMAR

1. Aim: to ask the students to figure out for themselves the difference between *will* and *going to*.
- Go through the conversation line by line with the students and ask them to decide when the decision was made.

> **Answer**
> You use *going to* for decisions made before the moment of speaking and *will* for decisions made at the moment of speaking.

- Ask the students to read the information about *going to* for plans in the grammar box.

2. Aim: to focus on things which are sure to happen and things which are not so sure.
- Suggest to the students that they use their answers to *Listening* activity 3 to do this activity. Make sure the students use *going to* for things which are sure to happen and *will probably* for things which are not so sure.

> **Answers**
> He's going to fly to Rio.
> He'll probably take the cable car up the mountain.
> He's going to fly to Santiago.
> He'll probably do some sightseeing.
> He's going to lie on the beach in Valparaiso.
> He's going to meet his girlfriend in Lima.
> They're going to visit the ruins in Machu Picchu.
> They'll probably go somewhere in the Amazon.
> They'll probably spend a week in the jungle.

3. Aim: to focus on the difference between *going to* and *will*.

> **Answers**
> 1. "I need a strong bag." "I **will** get you one."
> 2. I bought a good map, because **I'm going** to South America.
> 3. "Where **are you going to** stay?" "**We'll** stay with friends, probably."
> 4. I need some fresh air. I think **I'll** take a walk in the park.

SPEAKING AND VOCABULARY

1. Aim: to develop speaking skills.
- Ask the students to work in groups of two or three and to think of a place to visit. Try to make sure each group chooses somewhere different, and make sure they don't tell the other groups the place they have chosen.

2. Aim: to focus on the words in the vocabulary box.
- Ask the groups to think about the words in the box and decide which things they need to take with them. Ask them to add three or four more things.

3. Aim: to practice using *will* for decisions made at the moment of speaking.
- Ask the groups to decide who will get each thing. Make sure everyone uses *will* for a decision made at the moment of speaking.

4. Aim: to practice using *going to* for decisions made before the moment of speaking.
- Ask the students to check who is going to get which things. Make sure they use *going to* for decisions made before the moment of speaking. Remind them, if necessary, that they made the decision in activity 3.

- You can finish this activity sequence by asking one group to write the list of things it needs for the trip on the board. The others must try to guess where they are going and what they are going to do there. The group can only answer *yes* or *no* to any questions:
Are you going somewhere in South America? No.
Are you going somewhere in Asia? Yes.
Are you going to the beach?
When the class has guessed where the group is going, they can ask five more questions.

- Make sure each group has a turn at writing their list of things on the board.

14

GENERAL COMMENTS

Prepositions; asking for and giving directions

In contrast to Lesson 13, the grammar and functions in this lesson will pose the students less of a problem. They will already have used prepositions of place in a number of lessons in *Move Up* Student's Book, and may have studied asking for and giving directions in a previous course.

All That Jazz

The title of this lesson is an expression which basically means "and so on," but is an appropriate lead-in to a walking tour of some of the jazz clubs in the French Quarter of New Orleans (pronounced *NAWlins* or *NORlyuns*.) The seven clubs mentioned in this text are a tiny percentage of the total number of music clubs in the city, which richly deserves to be called the birthplace of jazz. Due to the mixture of ethnicities in New Orleans, the pronunciation of some of the street and place names is a little idiosyncratic: New Orleans itself is commonly pronounced /ˈnalɪns/, Louis /ˈluːɪs/, Chartres /ˈtʃardərz/, Toulouse /ˈtuːluːs/, Decatur /dəˈkeɪdər/, and Conti /ˈkantaɪ/.

VOCABULARY AND READING

1. **Aim: to present the vocabulary in the box; to distinguish between parts of speech.**
- Ask the students to underline the adjectives in the box.

> **Answers**
> real, famous, traditional, happy, tired, atmospheric

2. **Aim: to present the words in the vocabulary box.**
- Ask the students to look at the map and to try to find examples of the words in the box.

> **Answers**
> cathedral: St. Louis Cathedral
> river: Mississippi River
> square: Jackson Square
> concert hall: Municipal Auditorium
> market: French Market
> theater: New Orleans Theater for the Performing Arts
> park: Louis Armstrong Park
> aquarium: Aquarium of the Americas

- You may like to ask students to say if the features mentioned in the box can be found in their own town, and if so, where.

3. **Aim: to read and follow directions from a text.**
- Explain to the students that they are going to read a guided tour of the jazz bars in a famous area of New Orleans, Louisiana. The passage is written in a spoken style, so that although the directions are not precise, they are the kind that a tourist in an American city might hear.

- Ask the students to locate the starting point of this tour, near the French Market on Decatur Street. Make sure that they know where north is on the map, and that "left" and "right" are relative to what their position would be if they were actually walking through the French Quarter.

- Ask the students to read the text and draw the route on the map in their books. Ask them to fill in the names of the clubs in the appropriate spaces on the map.

- When the students have finished, ask them to check their answers in pairs.

> **Answers**
> 1. Palm Court Café
> 2. Maxwell's Toulouse Cabaret
> 3. Preservation Hall
> 4. Maison Bourbon Nite Club
> 5. Famous Door Jazz Café
> 6. Famous Door
> 7. Jazz Meridien

GRAMMAR

1. **Aim: to focus on the use of prepositions of place.**
- Ask the students to look at the information on prepositions of place and asking for and giving directions in the grammar box.

- Ask the students to do the exercise.

> **Possible Answers**
> Jackson Brewery is on the corner of Decatur Street and St. Peter's.
> The World Trade Center is between Poydras Street and the Mississippi River.
> Clinton Street is in front of Decatur Street.
> Canal Place is on Canal Street.
> New Orleans Theater for the Performing Arts is behind Louis Armstrong Park.

2. **Aim: to practice writing and reading directions.**
- Ask the students to locate Jackson Square on the map. Tell them to find another location on the map, but not to tell anyone which location they have chosen.

- Ask them to write directions from Jackson Square to the secret location. Go around and check that their directions are clear and correct.

- When they have finished, ask them to exchange directions with a partner, and then to read and find the secret location.

SOUNDS

1. **Aim: to practice /æ/, /ə/, /ɑː/, and /eɪ/.**
- 📼 Each of these sounds can be represented by the letter "a" which can be very confusing to students whose native language has a more phonetic writing system than English. The different pronunciations are important in conveying the meaning of the word, however, and students should learn the correct pronunciation along with the word itself.

- Point out that the letter "a" is always pronounced /ə/ when it occurs in an unstressed syllable.

> **Answers**
> /æ/: atmospheric fan half happy jazz
> /ə/: across agree aquarium away final
> /ɑː/: start
> /eɪ/: famous place take

2. **Aim: to focus on word stress in questions.**
- Ask the students to predict which words are likely to be stressed. Remind them, if necessary, that the stressed words in a sentence are the words the speaker considers to be important.

- 📼 Play the tape and ask the students to check their answers. Pause the tape so they can ask the questions out loud.

> **Answers**
> 1. Excuse me, how do I get to the bus station?
> 2. Pardon me, is there a bank near here?
> 3. Excuse me, could you tell me where the market is?
> 4. Pardon me, where's the nearest police station?

SPEAKING

1. **Aim: to practice using prepositions of place.**
- Ask the students to work in pairs and follow the pairwork instructions. Remind them to use some of the prepositions in the grammar and functions box.

2. **Aim: to practice giving directions.**
- Ask the students to work in pairs and to turn to their instructions in the Communication Activities section on pages 58 and 60. Make sure they realize they can use the map of New Orleans.

- If both students in each pair come from a town they know well, they can continue this activity by describing the route from one well-known place to another, without saying where they are going. The student who is listening must follow the route in his or her head. They can prepare this activity for homework; ask the students to write a guided tour. Then at the beginning of the next lesson, spend five minutes asking the students to read other people's guided tours and to follow the route in their heads.

15

GENERAL COMMENTS

Countable and uncountable nouns

Countable (or count) nouns and uncountable (or mass) nouns often cause students some difficulties. It's not always obvious from the noun if it is countable or uncountable. Sometimes a word can have a countable meaning in one context and an uncountable one in another (country, cold, wine, chicken), and logic doesn't necessarily help the student decide. While this lesson was being piloted, one student was extremely confused to be told that *money* is uncountable! (Money is uncountable because you cannot have two monies, although you can have two dollars.) It is important to treat the matter as an issue of vocabulary, and to encourage students to annotate each new word and meaning as C or U.

Jigsaw listening

This is a technique in which a class is divided into three groups. Each group is given a cassette containing a third of a listening passage (each group having a different third), and a cassette player, and is asked to listen to their part of the passage. They then work together to check that they have all understood their part. Then members of each group form a new group and reconstitute the passage as a whole. The technique is effective in pedagogical terms in that it creates an information gap between members of the new group (you know something I don't, I know something you don't) which is central to communicative language teaching. But there are practical problems: a teacher may not have three cassette players, or may not have the space to allow three groups to work separately. In this lesson, there is a jigsaw listening activity with one tape recorder, in which students work in groups of three, all listening to the same passage, but for different information. The information gap is not as tight, but teachers who have tried the technique agree that it is sufficient to generate a highly motivated sharing of information.

VOCABULARY

1. Aim: to present the words in the vocabulary box.

● This activity is designed to present the new words to the students and to encourage them to put them into personalized categories. There may be too many items to learn, but it is to be expected that by the end of the *Vocabulary* activities, they will have been exposed to and have understood all of the words, and will probably retain the words they have placed in the *every day* and *twice a week* categories.

● Ask the students to categorize the words under the headings. Encourage them to think of two or three other items to add to the list, so that the vocabulary acquisition process is supported by the personal relevance of the words to be retained.

● Ask one or two students what they eat *every day* and *never*. Then ask other students to compare their lists.

2. Aim: to practice using the new words.

Possible Answers
apples, bananas, cabbage, fruit, grapes, onions, oranges, peaches, vegetables.
Other fruit and vegetables in the photo are: beans, blackberries, blueberries, broccoli, melons, pears, peppers, pineapples, pumpkins, raspberries.

3. Aim: to present some common words to describe quantity.

● Ask the students to look at the words in the box and the examples below. Ask the class *Can you buy a bottle of apples? Can you buy a can of bananas?* and find someone who says *no*.

● Write the words in the box on the board as headings, and ask students to come and write the food words under the suitable headings.

Possible Answers
bottle: beer, juice, milk, oil, water, wine
can: carrots, fruit, peaches, peas, tomatoes
cup: coffee, tea
glass: beer, juice, milk, water, wine
loaf: bread
package: butter, cheese, coffee, cookies, pasta, rice, tea
piece: bread, cheese, fruit
pound: butter, coffee, pasta, rice, tea, (and all the fruit, vegetables, and meat, but not bread and liquids)
slice: beef, bread, cheese, chicken, fruit, ham, lamb, meat, onion, orange, peach, pork, tomato

● The answers depend on the item in question, whether it is liquid or solid, and on matters of usage. For example, we don't talk about *a glass of coffee* because we don't serve coffee in a glass. *Cup* is used as a measurement in American English, and so it can be used with all the words that you can use *pound* with. There will be other combinations in certain contexts which are not covered by the answers above.

● Say a food item, e.g. *flour* and elicit the response *a package of flour*. Try this with several food items.

● If you have time, use the activity for some cross-cultural awareness. Would the students say in their language *a glass of coffee, a package of cheese, a slice of potato, a cup of wine, a pound of bread*?

GRAMMAR

1. Aim: to focus on whether items of food and drink are countable or uncountable.

● Ask the students to read the information about expressions of quantity in the grammar box and then do the exercise.

● It was mentioned in the introduction that some words can be either countable or uncountable, depending on the context. Generally speaking an uncountable noun becomes countable when you talk about a kind or variety of things, e.g. *Chilean wines are among the best in the world*. The answers below refer to the context of food and drink, and shopping.

Answers
apples C, bananas C, beef U, beer U, bread U, butter U, cabbage U, carrots C, cheese U, chicken U, coffee U, cookies C, eggs C, fish U, fruit U, grapes C, ham U, juice U, lamb U, lettuce U, meat U, milk U, oil U, onions C, oranges C, pasta U, peaches C, peas C, pork U, potatoes C, rice U, salad U, strawberries C, tea U, tomatoes C, vegetables C, water U, wine U

2. Aim: to focus on *some, any, much,* and *many*.

● 🔲 Ask the students to complete the dialogue and then play the tape to check.

Answers
A We need **some** water. How **many** bottles do we need?
B Two. And we don't have **any** fruit. Do you want to get **some** peaches?
A OK. Do we have **any** coffee?
B No, how **much** do we need?
A Just one pound.

LISTENING AND SPEAKING

1. Aim: to pre-teach some difficult words from the listening passage.

● Make sure the students understand the food items. They can use their dictionaries if they wish. They should be able to understand most of the other vocabulary in the listening passage.

2. Aim: to listen for specific information.

● 🔲 Ask the students to work in three groups, A, B, and C. The members in each group should look at their instructions in the Communication Activities section. Each group has different instructions and different information to listen for. Ask them to listen and to write notes in answer to their specific questions. Point out to the students that Pat is a man, and is interviewed first.

● Ask the students to discuss their answers in groups, and check that everyone has got the same information.

3. Aim: to discuss what they have heard, to reconstitute the two listening passages, and to complete the chart.

● Ask the students to form new groups of three people, with one person from group A, one person from group B, and one person from group C. They should work together, and talk about the notes they made in activity 2. It may be that some students can remember information which they were not asked to write down. But the rule is that they can only talk about information which they were specifically asked to listen for and write down. Ask them to fill the chart in with as much detail as possible. They can copy the chart if there is not enough space in their books.

● You may like to check their answers to the chart by drawing it on the board and asking the students to fill it in orally.

Answers

	Pat	Karen
Typical breakfast	coffee, cereal, fruit juice	cereal, toast, orange juice, coffee
Typical lunch	pasta, vegetables, sub sandwich	sandwich, baked potato
Typical dinner	seafood, vegetables, salad, pie	Chinese, Japanese, Indonesian food, dumplings with meat and vegetables

4. Aim: to practice using the vocabulary and grammar presented in this lesson.

● Ask the students to talk about their typical meals and to complete the *You* column of the chart in activity 3.

5. Aim: to continue talking about eating habits; to practice using expressions of quantity.

● Explain that the expressions of quantity in the list are in a graded sequence from *a lot* to *not any*. You can do this activity with the class as a whole, simply asking them for their reactions to Karen's and Pat's eating habits, using some of the expressions.

6. Aim: to continue talking about eating habits.

● Ask the students to write a list of ten things they often eat and drink.

● Ask the students to go around asking people if they eat and drink the same things, like this: *Do you eat cheese? Yes, I do. I drink wine. So do I.* Even in a mono-cultural class there will be plenty of small differences.

● Ask the students to find out how much they eat, drink, or use. Check that they are using *how much* with uncountable nouns and *how many* with countable nouns.

● You may like to ask the students to write a brief report on the class's eating and drinking habits for homework.

Fluency 3

GENERAL COMMENTS

This lesson focuses on money, prices, and the cost of living. It presents the opportunity for students to review numbers, which they will have learned in earlier classes. Usually, the greatest difficulty students have is receptive – when they hear numbers they find it difficult to decipher them as quickly as they might in their own language. You might like to give them further practice during this lesson and on other occasions in hearing and writing down numbers.

VOCABULARY AND SPEAKING

Aim: to present the items of vocabulary in the box; to practice speaking.

● This activity is designed to introduce the theme of the lesson and some of its essential vocabulary. Make sure everyone understands what the words in the box mean. Translate them if necessary.

● Ask the students to work in pairs and to talk about how much they or their parents spend on each item.

● Ask the students to go around and find out how other students have answered the question.

SPEAKING AND LISTENING

1. **Aim: to prepare for listening; to focus on the content of a listening passage.**

● Ask the students to read the passage and to think about where they might hear it and whether a similar customer-service situation might take place in their country. Focus on the differences—the choice of packaging for the cigarettes, the self-service, etc.

2. **Aim: to practice listening for specific information.**

● 📼 Tell the students they are going to listen to the dialogue but that they are going to hear some slight differences. They should underline the phrases which are different.

Answers	
CLERK	<u>Hi there.</u> What can I do for you?
MAN	I'd like a pack of Marlboro, please.
CLERK	Soft pack or box?
MAN	Box, please.
CLERK	<u>There you are,</u> one pack of Marlboros. That's two-fifty. <u>Will that be all for you today, sir?</u>
MAN	Oh, I need a gallon of milk.
CLERK	<u>Right over there in the refrigerator, sir. Help yourself.</u>
MAN	Right. And do you have today's paper?
CLERK	<u>We sure do.</u> That's fifty cents... and three twenty-nine for the milk, two-fifty for the Marlboro. That's six twenty-nine altogether, sir.
MAN	<u>Here you are.</u>
CLERK	Out of ten? That's thirty, forty, fifty, <u>seven dollars, eight, nine, and ten.</u>
MAN	Thanks.
CLERK	<u>Thank you, sir.</u> Have a nice day.

3. **Aim: to practice speaking.**

● Ask the students to work in pairs and discuss which phrases were different. They can rewrite the dialogue with as many details as they can remember.

● 📼 Play the tape again and ask the students to check their answers in pairs.

● Ask the students to act out the dialogue they heard (not the one they can read in 2).

● Ask two or three pairs to act out the dialogue in front of the class.

4. **Aim: to practice speaking.**

● Ask the students to act out this role play using the dialogue in 1 to help them. Ask Student B to think of three or four things he or she wants to buy. Student A should be ready with suitable prices.

● Ask two or three pairs to act out their dialogues in front of the class.

FUNCTIONS

1. Aim: to practice saying numbers.

● Ask the students to read the information in the functions box and do this activity on their own.

● 📼 Play the tape and ask the students to check their answers in pairs.

> **Answers**
> 1. a 2. b 3. b 4. a

2. Aim: to focus on weak and strong syllable stress in numbers.

● Remind the students that the pronunciation of the "teens" (13–19) and the tens (30–90) is very similar and mistakes can often be made.

● Ask the students to say the words out loud and to underline the stressed syllable.

● 📼 Play the tape and ask the students to listen and check.

> **Answers**
> thirteen   thirty
> fourteen   forty
> seventeen   seventy
> nineteen   ninety
> thirteen dollars   fourteen feet
> seventeen hours   nineteen miles

3. Aim: to practice listening to and writing down numbers.

● 📼 Your students are likely to find this activity quite difficult, so play the tape several times or stop after every number and check that they've been able to do it.

> **Answers**
> $10.50
> 12,314
> 204
> $19.99
> 138,526
> $20.50

● Ask the students to say the numbers out loud.

SPEAKING AND LISTENING 2

1. Aim: to practice speaking; to prepare for listening.

● If your students are quite young, it may be that they don't know how much the items cost in their country. You may need to be sure that you know the right answers before you come to the class!

● Ask the students to talk about how much things cost in groups of three.

2. Aim: to practice speaking and listening.

● This is a jigsaw listening activity in which each student listens to the same tape but for different information. They are then asked to complete the chart, each contributing the piece of information they have noted down.

● 📼 At this stage everyone is working on their own. You could make the activity easier at this stage by putting two or three Students A together, two or three Students B together, etc. Make sure everyone understands what they should listen for. Then play the tape.

3. Aim: to practice speaking.

● At this stage, the students work with members of their original group again. They should work together and complete the chart.

4. Aim: to practice speaking.

● Use this opportunity to compare prices and the cost of living in different countries.

● You may like to ask the students to write a short passage in answer to the question in this activity for homework.

Progress Check 11–15

GENERAL COMMENTS

You can work through this Progress Check in the order shown, or concentrate on areas which may have caused difficulty in Lessons 11 to 15. You can also let the students choose the activities which they would like to, or feel the need to do.

VOCABULARY

1. Aim: to present word maps as a way of remembering and organizing new vocabulary.
- Word maps can be useful devices to consolidate the acquisition of new ideas and to organize vocabulary into vocabulary fields. The students should do this activity on their own.

- Ask the students to compare their word maps.

2. Aim: to focus on noun suffixes.
- Explain that suffixes often indicate the part of speech of a new word. For example, *-er* is often used for the names of people or things that do something. This activity focuses on the suffixes which often indicate jobs.

> **Answers**
> **verbs:** act, bank, dance, manage, teach, write
> **nouns:** bank, dance, journal, music, politics

3. Aim: to help students organize their vocabulary learning.
- You may want to suggest that the students extend their *Wordbanks* beyond the space available in the Practice Book.

GRAMMAR

1. Aim: to review questions with *going to*.

> **Answers**
> 1. Is she going to be an accountant?
> 2. Is she going to live in the United States?
> 3. Is she going to start her own company?
> 4. Is she going to learn Portuguese?
> 5. Is she going to visit South America?
> 6. Is she going to start a new life?

2. Aim: to review *going to*.

> **Answers**
> 1. No, she isn't. She's going to be a doctor.
> 2. No, she isn't. She's going to move to Canada.
> 3. No, she isn't. She's going to work in a hospital.
> 4. No, she isn't. She's going to learn Spanish.
> 5. No, she isn't. She's going to travel around Spain.
> 6. No, she isn't. She's going to stay in contact with her old friends.

3. Aim: to review *going to*.
- The students should write their own answers to these questions.

4. Aim: to review *going to* and *would like to*.

> **Answers**
> 1. He's got his ticket and he's **going to** fly to São Paulo.
> 2. I'**d like to** buy a car, but I don't have any money.
> 3. It's **going to** rain today.
> 4. We'**d like to** go on a vacation but we're too busy.
> 5. He has his coat on and he's **going to** leave now.
> 6. We sold our apartment last week and we're **going to** live abroad.

5. Aim: to review *will* and *going to*.

> **Answers**
> 1. It's too early. Maybe I'**ll** go back to bed.
> 2. He's **going to** fly to Rio next week.
> 3. She's **going to** have a baby next July.
> 4. "I'm so tired." "I'**ll** take you home by car."
> 5. He has just gotten a job in Caracas, so he's **going to** move there.
> 6. Maybe we'**ll** have dinner in a restaurant.

6. Aim: to review making predictions.
- The students should write their own sentences.

7. Aim: to review the use of prepositions.
- The students can write their own sentences.

8. Aim: to review giving directions.
- The students should write their own directions.

9. Aim: to review countable and uncountable nouns.

> **Answers**
> egg C, money U, orange juice U, apple C, sugar U, potato C, butter U, rice U, strawberry C, cheese U

10. Aim: to review *How much* and *How many*?

> **Answers**
> How many eggs do you have?
> How much money do you have?
> How much orange juice do you have?
> How many apples do you have?
> How much sugar do you have?
> How many potatoes do you have?
> How much butter do you have?
> How much rice do you have?
> How many strawberries do you have?
> How much cheese do you have?

- Check that the students form the irregular plurals properly, *potatoes* and *strawberries*.

11. Aim: to review *some* and *any*.

> **Answers**
> 1. Do you have **any** oranges?
> 2. I'd like **some** wine, please.
> 3. I don't have **any** money with me.
> 4. Is there **any** water?
> 5. We have **some** chicken, but we don't have **any** salad.
> 6. I'll get you **some** bread, if you want.

SOUNDS

1. Aim: to review the sound /ə/.
- The students have already practiced the /ə/ sound in Lesson 9. Ask them to say the words.

- 🔊 Play the tape and ask the students to listen and check.

> **Answers**
> pizza polite police America company opera
> performance potato national

2. Aim: to practice the sounds /tʃ/ and /ʃ/.
- Ask the students to say the words out loud.

- 🔊 Play the tape and ask the students to listen and check.

> **Answers**
> /tʃ/: charm chicken cheese peach
> /ʃ/: politician traditional she old-fashioned fish

3. Aim: to practice contrastive stress.
- 🔊 Make sure the students understand that they are going to respond to the prompts on tape with the same sentence, but stressing a different word each time. Play the tape and stop it at each pause.

> **Answers**
> 1. No, **Joe** is going to study math at the university.
> 2. No, Joe is going to study **math** at the university.
> 3. No, Joe is going to study math at the **university**.
> 4. No, Joe is **going** to study math at the university.

4. Aim: to focus on polite intonation.
- 🔊 Even in transactional situations, such as in a store or at the train station, American people try to sound polite. The intonation of a sentence can make a major contribution to how polite a speaker sounds; other factors would include the language the speaker uses.

> **Answers**
> 1. How do I get to the station?
> 2. How do I get to the hospital? ✔
> 3. Could you tell me where the city hall is? ✔
> 4. Could you tell me where the bus station is?
> 5. Where's the post office?
> 6. Where's the river? ✔

- Although it isn't the aim of cross-cultural training to make students acquire the behavior of a foreign culture, it is nevertheless designed to help them be sensitive to people from other cultures. Tell your students that in the United States it is important to sound as polite as possible, even to strangers. Repeating these sentences is not designed to make the students acquire American behavior, but to be aware of how intonation can change the way something may be perceived by someone.

SPEAKING

1. Aim: to provide speaking practice.
- Ask the students to plan the lunch they are going to arrange. They should decide the dish they are going to make and the place where they are going to have lunch. Go around the class and check that everyone is using *going to* and *will* correctly.

2. Aim: to practice writing a note with directions.
- Ask each student to choose someone from another group and to write to him or her saying where they're going to have lunch, and how to get there.

3. Aim: to practice using *will* for decisions and the vocabulary of food.
- Tear some paper into small pieces and give five pieces to each pair of students. Ask them to write one of the main ingredients for the meal on each piece of paper.

4. Aim: to practice using the vocabulary of food.
- Collect all the pieces of paper with the ingredients, shuffle them, and then give out five new pieces of paper to each pair of students. These pieces of paper will obviously not have the ingredients the students wrote in activity 3. The students' task is to find the ingredients they need for their meal, using the language shown in the example. The only rule is that if someone asks for an ingredient, the other person must hand it over even if he or she needs it.

- Each student should check with his or her partner now and then. When they have got the ingredients for their meal, they have won. (It doesn't matter if they have pieces of paper which they didn't originally write; only the ingredients matter.)

16

GENERAL COMMENTS

Prepositions of time and place

The students have already been using prepositions of time and place in *Move Up* Pre-intermediate. This lesson is designed to consolidate and organize their knowledge of this grammar point.

Cross-cultural training

The theme of this lesson is entertainment in different countries. It is not the aim of *Move Up* to give extensive and specific information about different cultures because that would involve much more time and space than is available. The aim is to present aspects of certain *sample* cultures with which the students can compare their culture.

Jigsaw listening

There is another example of jigsaw listening with one tape recorder. For details of the rationale behind this technique, see the General Comments in Lesson 15.

VOCABULARY

Aim: to present the words in the vocabulary box.

● Ask the students how they like to spend their spare time. Write their hobbies and interests on the board and put a check by each one for each student who enjoys it. Which is the most popular hobby or interest in the class?

● On the board write *What's on?* and *Where?* and to illustrate their meaning, suggest a film or a play which is on in your town and then say where. Go around the class asking students to suggest what's on in their town and where it's taking place.

● Ask the students to put the words in the box under the headings. They can do this on the board and then copy the lists into their notebooks.

● Explain that not all of the words can go into the two categories, and should be put into a third category, *Related words*. Tell the students that some related words can go with more than one category. Ask them to continue their work until they have categorized all the words in the vocabulary box. They may like to do this stage in pairs.

Answers		
What's on?	**Where?**	**Related words**
ballet	opera house, theater	ticket, row, seat, performance, intermission
concert	opera house, theater	ticket, row, seat, performance, intermission
disco	club	ticket
exhibition	gallery, museum	painting, ticket, closing time, opening hours, sculpture
game	stadium	ticket, row, seat, intermission
movie	movie theater	ticket, row, seat
musical	theater	ticket, row, seat, performance, intermission
opera	opera house	ticket, row, seat, performance, intermission
play	theater	ticket, row, seat, performance, intermission
show	theater	ticket, row, seat, performance, intermission

● Explain that you talk about an *exhibition of sculpture* or *paintings*.

● Ask the students to decide which of the words they can use to talk about their hobbies and interests.

LISTENING AND SPEAKING

1. Aim: to listen for specific information.

● 🔊 Ask the students to work in three groups, A, B, and C. The members in each group should look at their instructions in the Communication Activities section. Each group has different instructions and different information to listen for. Ask them to listen and to write notes in answer to their specific questions.

● Ask the students in each group to discuss their answers, and check that everyone has got the same information.

2. Aim: to discuss what they have heard, to reconstitute the two listening passages, and to complete the chart.

● Ask the students to form new groups of three people, with one person from group A, one person from group B, and one person from group C. They should work together, and talk about the notes they made in activity 1. Remember (from Lesson 15) the rule is that they can only talk about information which they were specifically asked to listen for and write down. Ask them to fill the chart in with as much detail as possible. They can copy the chart if there is not enough space in their books.

● You may like to check their answers to the chart by drawing it on the board and asking the students to fill it in orally.

3. **Aim: to practice speaking about types of entertainment.**

● The students should now be ready to talk about a typical entertainment in their country. If they are all from the same country, ask them to suggest typical types of entertainment, and to talk about each one using the chart to help them.

● Alternatively, ask the students to work in small groups and to copy and complete the chart, but leave out the name of the entertainment. When they are ready, ask them to tell other groups about the place, performers, type of music, and the reasons why people enjoy it, and ask them to guess what the type of entertainment is.

GRAMMAR AND FUNCTIONS

1. **Aim: to focus on prepositions of time and place.**
● Ask the students to read the information about prepositions of time and place and making invitations and suggestions in the grammar and functions box.

● This activity is simply another way of organizing the information in the grammar and functions box.

2. **Aim: to focus on the prepositions you use to talk about time.**

3. **Aim: to practice using prepositions of time and place.**

● In 2 it is possible to say *in the Metropolitan Gallery*, which stresses that the exhibition is inside the building. *At* refers to the Metropolitan Gallery as a location.

4. **Aim: to practice making, accepting, and refusing invitations.**
● This activity involves some movement around the class. If this is not possible, the students can ask their nearest neighbors without leaving their seats. The students should begin the activity with a blank appointments diary, and complete parts of it as they accept invitations.

● You may like to explain that if you refuse an invitation, an American would expect you to give an explanation. Ask the students if this is the case in their cultures.

WRITING

1. **Aim: to practice writing an invitation.**
● Ask the students to look at the invitation and find out what's on, where, and when. You can write this information on the board.

● The students should then copy out the letter and complete it with the information on the board.

2. **Aim: to practice accepting or refusing a written invitation.**
● Ask the students to work in pairs and to exchange invitations. Ask them to write a reply to the invitation, using the layout of the letter as a model.

● Remind the students to include their address at the top of the letter, the date, to write *Dear* (name), and to finish it *Best wishes* and their name. Point out that this is an informal way of closing a letter.

● If there isn't much time left, the students can do this activity for homework.

Preparation for Lesson 17
● Ask the students to bring some magazine photos of some famous people for Lesson 17.

17

GENERAL COMMENTS

Describing appearance and character

Some students may be shy or embarrassed about describing their or other people's appearance and character. If you think this is likely with your group, you may like to bring some magazine photos of people which can be used for description instead of other people in the class.

Paintings

portraits: Left hand side, top: *Jeanne Hebuterne* by Amadeo Modigliani (1884–1920, Italian); middle: *Self portrait* by Vincent van Gogh (1853–90, Dutch); bottom: *The Girl With a Red Hat* by Jan Vermeer (1632–1675, Dutch); right hand side: *Self portrait* by Stanley Spencer (1891–1959, English)

Optional extra material

Magazine photos of people. (See above.)

VOCABULARY

1. **Aim: to focus on the words in the vocabulary box and to distinguish between parts of speech.**

   ● Ask the students to look at the list of words and simply choose any which they could use to describe themselves.

   ● You can ask the students to tell you about their choice of words, or you can move onto the next stage.

   ● Ask the students to separate the nouns from the adjectives in two lists.

   > **Answers**
   > **adjectives:** attractive, bald, beautiful, big, black, blond, brown, curly, dark, fair, good-looking, kind, long, medium-height, middle-aged, nice, old, overweight, pretty, round, short, shy, slim, square, straight, tall, thin, ugly, young
   > **nouns:** beard, face, glasses, hair, head, man, moustache, teenager, woman

   ● You may need to point out that to describe someone as *overweight* or *fat* or *ugly* is very direct and potentially rather rude in many cultures. People may also be sensitive about being *bald, old,* and *short,* so the words are presented here mainly for receptive use. *Pretty* is usually used only for girls and women, and *good-looking* mostly for men.

   ● Ask the students to group words which often go together. This collocation activity will be very useful during the rest of the lesson.

> **Possible Answers**
> **beard:** black, blond, curly, dark, fair, long, short
> **face:** attractive, beautiful, kind, long, nice, pretty, round, square, thin, ugly
> **glasses:** dark, round, square
> **hair:** attractive, beautiful, black, blond, brown, curly, dark, fair, long, nice, pretty, short, straight, thin
> **head:** bald
> **man/teenager:** attractive, black, blond, dark, fair, good-looking, kind, middle-aged, old, overweight, nice, short, shy, slim, tall, thin, ugly, young
> **woman/teenager:** attractive, beautiful, black, blond, dark, fair, good-looking, kind, middle-aged, old, overweight, nice, pretty, short, shy, slim, tall, thin, ugly, young

● Only do the last stage of the activity if the students had difficulty with the collocation work.

> **Answers**
> **height:** short, medium-height, tall
> **age:** middle-aged, old, teenager, young
> **looks:** attractive, beautiful, good-looking, pretty, ugly
> **build:** big, overweight, round, slim, thin
> **character:** kind, nice, shy

● You may like to put the collocations and the final grouping on the board to refer to during the lesson.

2. **Aim: to practice using the words in the vocabulary box.**

   ● Ask the students to suggest the name of a famous person. Make sure everyone knows this person, then ask them to suggest adjectives chosen from the box to describe the person.

   ● Ask the students to think of a famous person, or to choose someone from the magazine photos, if you have brought some in. They should follow the instructions in the book.

FUNCTIONS

1. Aim: to focus on the use of *like* for appearance and character.

● Ask the students to read the information about describing appearance and character in the functions box.

● Ask the students to do the exercise.

> **Answers**
> 1. What does she look **like?** She looks – very kind.
> 2. Who's she **like?** She's **like** her mother.
> 3. What's he **like?** He's – wonderful!
> 4. Who does he look **like?** He looks **like** his brother.

2. Aim: to focus on questions and answers about personal appearance.

● Ask the students to do this on their own and then check their answers orally.

> **Answers**
> 1. d   2. a   3. b   4. c

3. Aim: to practice describing appearance and character; to present *kind of, very,* and *really.*

● Ask the students to use the language in the box to describe members of their family and friends. You may need to explain that in this context *kind of* means *fairly.* There is a chance that a student will have heard *kind of* used to mean *a type of,* e.g. *There are three kinds of cheese.*

SPEAKING

1. Aim: to practice describing people's appearance.

● Ask the students to work in pairs. Choose someone in the paintings and describe him or her. Ask the students to point to the person you're describing. Go around and check that they are pointing to the right person.

● Ask the students to choose someone in the paintings and describe him or her to their partners. The other student must guess who is being described.

2. Aim: to practice describing people's character.

● Ask the students to imagine that they can meet the people in the paintings. Ask them to think about who they would like to meet and why. You can do this activity with the whole class.

● You can extend activities 1 and 2 with the magazine photos, if the students have brought any.

WRITING

1. Aim: to prepare for writing a letter describing your appearance.

● If your students chose adjectives to describe themselves at the beginning of *Vocabulary* activity 1, ask them to write them down. If they did not, ask them to choose adjectives now and write them down. If you have got a class with a sense of humor, you can ask them to choose adjectives that would describe how they would like to look!

2. Aim: to write sentences about your appearance.

● Ask the students to write full sentences describing their appearance.

3. Aim: to practice joining sentences.

● Ask the students to join the sentences using *and.* You may need to help them choose the best sentences to join. Usually, we only join a couple of sentences with *and,* and then perhaps add a phrase beginning *with,* as in *I'm in my mid-twenties and I'm kind of tall with brown hair.*

4. Aim: to write a letter describing your appearance.

● Ask the students to rewrite their sentences in the form of a letter, using the model provided. Make sure they put their address at the top, with the date, begin with *Dear...,* and end *Yours sincerely.* Explain this is a formal letter to someone you don't know, so it is less usual to use contractions.

18

GENERAL COMMENTS

Average age

This lesson continues the theme of describing character begun in Lesson 17.

Making comparisons (1)

This is the first of three lessons about making comparisons. This lesson focuses on the comparative and superlative forms of adjectives. The rules for this are a little complicated and if this is the first time your students have done this, you may need to give further practice using material from *Move Up* Practice Book and the Resource Pack. There is also a more detailed explanation in the Grammar Review at the back of the Student's Book.

VOCABULARY

1. Aim: to present the words in the vocabulary box.

● Ask the students to choose five words from the box to describe themselves. Then ask one or two of them to tell the class about their choice of words. It is best to choose the more extrovert students for this task and it is important for the atmosphere to remain lighthearted.

● Ask the students to think of other words to describe themselves. They can use their dictionaries for this activity.

● Ask the students to work in pairs and to discuss their choice of words.

● Ask one or two pairs about their choice of words and discuss these choices with the rest of the class. Once again, it is important to choose students who are not shy about discussing their personalities.

2. Aim: to practice using the new words.

● This activity is a game which is not intended to be taken too seriously. The communication activity will reveal that the words the students chose to describe the first person show the kind of person they'd like to be. The words they chose for the second person show how they think other people see them. The words they chose to describe the third person show their true character!

● Ask the students to follow the instructions, choosing three famous people and three sets of adjectives to describe these people.

● Before you tell the students to turn to the Communication Activity, ask one or two people to tell you the names of the people and the adjectives they chose. Write them on the board.

● Now tell them to turn to Communication Activity 8 on page 59.

READING

1. Aim: to read and react to a passage.

● The passage concerns a subject which everyone has some experience of. It is their own general knowledge and experience which provides the reading comprehension check. You may want to let the students use a dictionary.

2. Aim: to discuss reactions to the passage.

● When the students have read the passage, ask them to discuss their reactions and decide which is the most surprising piece of information. If, at any stage, you think the students may need a comparative or superlative adjective, work through the *Grammar* section before doing this activity.

● Broaden the discussion by asking the students if they know of any exceptional old or young people.

GRAMMAR

1. Aim: to focus on the formation of comparative and superlative adjectives.

● Ask the students to read the information about making comparisons in the grammar box.

● Ask the students to do the activity.

> **Answers**
> kind kinder kindest
> nice nicer nicest
> lazy lazier laziest
> sad sadder saddest
> careful more careful most careful
>
> The rule for forming the comparative and superlative forms of short adjectives ending in:
> *-e:* add *-r, -st*
> *-y:* drop the *-y* and add *-ier, -iest*
> **a vowel and a consonant:** double the consonant and add *-er, -est*
>
> The rule for forming the comparative and superlative forms of longer adjectives:
> *more, most* + adjective

● The students may want to look at the explanation in the Grammar Review at this stage.

2. Aim: to focus on the formation of comparative and superlative adjectives.

> **Answers**
> cold colder coldest
> imaginative more imaginative most imaginative
> intelligent more intelligent most intelligent
> healthy healthier healthiest
> tidy tidier tidiest
> beautiful more beautiful most beautiful
> polite more polite most polite
> patient more patient most patient
> young younger youngest
> funny funnier funniest
> nervous more nervous most nervous
> warm warmer warmest
> old older oldest

3. Aim: to practice speaking and using comparative and superlative adjectives.

● Ask the students to continue their discussion about the best age to do things. If you like, you can extend this activity so that the students not only suggest the best age to do things, but also suggest the reasons why.

SPEAKING

1. Aim: to prepare to talk about exceptional people, places, and things.

● The students can choose from the adjectives in *Grammar* activity 2, or from the adjectives in the vocabulary box to fill in the blanks in the questions.

2. Aim: to practice talking about exceptional people, places, and things.

● Ask the students to work in groups, asking their questions and answering other people's questions. They should write down the answers if possible.

19

GENERAL COMMENTS

Making comparisons (2)

This lesson is the second of three lessons about making comparisons. The first was Lesson 18 and the third is Book B, Lesson 15. This lesson deals with the words which you use with adjectives to make comparisons, e.g. *than, as,* etc.

Clothes

The words for clothes and colors in the vocabulary box are likely to be the most useful ones for most students. However, the vocabulary field is a broad one, and you may wish to extend the coverage beyond the items suggested.

Cross-cultural training

The choice of India to illustrate styles of clothing in a different country is, to a certain extent, an arbitrary one, but it creates the opportunity for cross-cultural comparison. In this context, it is a sample culture with which students can compare their own. It is not the intention to give the students a large amount of culture-specific information.

VOCABULARY

1. **Aim: to focus on the words in the vocabulary box.**
  ● This activity is designed to encourage the categorization of the words according to personal criteria. This will help make the words more relevant to the student and promote the learning process. Write the four categories on the board and start categorizing the words for yourself.

  ● Choose a student and guess how he or she would categorize the words. Find out if he or she agrees with you.

  ● Ask the students to put the words under the headings for themselves.

  ● You may like to ask people who know each other well to group the words for each other, and then find out if their partner agrees.

  ● Ask the students to add words to the list, and to group them under the new headings: *in winter, in summer, for work,* and *at home.*

2. **Aim: to present the words in the vocabulary box.**
  ● Continue the process of grouping the words according to personal criteria.

  ● Find out how many people in the class like the different colors. Which is the most and least popular color?

3. **Aim: to practice using the new vocabulary.**
  ● Ask the students to work in pairs and to talk about the clothes they and other people wear.

  ● Broaden the vocabulary work to a general discussion about clothes the students wear in different circumstances. Lead the discussion with the following questions: *Do all the students wear the same clothes in general, or is there anyone who is more or less formal? Do people like to blend in or stand out with the clothes they wear? Which is the most popular item of clothing?* You can do this activity in pairs and then finish it by finding out about the opinions of the class as a whole.

READING

1. **Aim: to read for specific information.**
  ● Explain that the reading passage is about clothing styles in India. Ask the students to say which nationality they think is shown in the photo.

  ● Ask the students to read and find out about clothes for work, traditional dress, and young people's fashions in India.

> **Answers**
> – clothes for work: nice clothes, but not suits and ties.
> – traditional dress: *sari* for women and the *achkan* suit for men on formal occasions, the *kurtha* suit for less formal occasions.
> – young people's fashions: jeans and T-shirts.

  ● Ask the students to compare their answers in pairs.

2. **Aim: to discuss clothing conventions.**
  ● Ask the class to talk about clothes for work, clothes at home, traditional dress, and young people's fashions in their country. You may want to give them some extra vocabulary at this stage. If they have traditional dress, how often and on which occasions do they wear it?

GRAMMAR AND FUNCTIONS

1. **Aim: to focus on the use of *as, than,* and *from* in making comparisons.**

● Ask the students to read the information about making comparisons in the grammar and functions box.

● Ask them to do the activity.

> **Answers**
> 1. He's much smarter **than** I am.
> 2. She's **as** intelligent **as** he is.
> 3. Her clothes are different **from** mine.
> 4. She has the same shoes **as** I have.
> 5. Sandals are less common here **than** in Florida.
> 6. Kids are more casual **than** their parents.

2. **Aim: to focus on *more* and *less*.**

> **Answers**
> 1. Yes, he's more formal than she is.
> 2. Yes, it's less quiet now than it was.
> 3. Yes, they're less expensive here than at home.
> 4. Yes, he's more pessimistic than she is.
> 5. Yes, it's less difficult to get good clothes here.
> 6. Yes, he's more nervous than she is.

3. **Aim: to practice making comparisons.**

● Ask the students to write sentences comparing what they wear with other people.

SOUNDS

1. **Aim: to focus on the unstressed pronunciation of *than, as,* and *from*.**

● 🔲 This activity is designed to draw the students' attention to the unstressed pronunciation of *than, as,* and *from*. Play the tape and pause after each sentence. Ask them to repeat the sentences.

2. **Aim: to focus on contrastive stress when disagreeing.**

● 🔲 There have already been some activities with contrastive stress in *Move Up* Pre-intermediate. This activity focuses on the stress and intonation pattern used when disagreeing over making comparisons. Play the tape.

● 🔲 Ask the students to work in pairs and to disagree with the statements. Rewind and play the tape again, pausing each time so they can check their answers.

LISTENING AND SPEAKING

1. **Aim: to prepare for listening.**

● Ask the students to read the statements and decide if they are true or false for their country. Ask one or two students for their reactions.

2. **Aim: to listen for main ideas.**

● 🔲 Explain to the students that they are going to listen to an American talking about conventions of clothing in the United States and that they should decide if the statements in activity 1 are true or false for the United States. Suggest that they check the statements which are true and put a cross by the statements which are false.

> **Answers**
> 1. Nice clothes aren't expensive.   ✔
> 2. Casual clothes are very expensive.   ✗
> 3. People are very formal.   ✗
> 4. Many people are kind of small.   ✗
> 5. The quality of clothes design is good. ✔

● You may want to play the passage a second time.

3. **Aim: to practice making comparisons.**

● This activity is designed to give some final practice in using comparative and superlative adjectives and making comparisons. Ask the students to discuss their answers to the questions.

● If there is no time, you can ask the students to write their answers to the questions for homework.

20

GENERAL COMMENTS

Numbers

Many speakers of a foreign language have difficulty in using numbers. Generally, it is more difficult to hear and write down numbers than to say them. With more extensive calculations, most people revert to their own language. So the aims of this lesson as far as numbers are concerned are modest. It is simply an opportunity to give some further practice in producing and receiving numbers. If your students need to be fluent in numbers, perhaps for professional reasons, you may have to supplement the work in *Move Up* Student's Book with activities from the Practice Book and the Resource Packs. You may also want to create further practice by making your own exercises using those in the Student's Book as a model.

Accuracy and fluency

Some teachers feel it is important for their students to be as accurate as possible on every occasion, and will correct every error a student makes. While accuracy is important in many exercises in *Move Up*, there are many discussion activities, especially in the *Speaking* sections, which are designed to promote fluency. On these occasions, it is better not to interrupt the communicative flow by correcting the students' mistakes. The criterion for correction on these occasions is intelligibility. If the student is intelligible, then it is better to make a note of the mistakes and draw the student's attention to them at the end of the activity.

VOCABULARY AND SOUNDS

1. **Aim: to present the words in the vocabulary box and to practice using them.**

● If there is time, write the words on the board. Ask the students to look at the photo. Ask one or two students to use the words to describe what they can see. Check the words as they use them.

2. **Aim: to practice saying longer numbers.**

● Ask the students to say the numbers out loud. You may want to extend this activity by writing some more numbers on the board, or asking students to work in pairs, writing numbers for each other and saying them out loud in turn.

● ▭ Play the tape and ask the students to listen and check. You may need to pause the tape after each number for the students to repeat.

LISTENING

1. **Aim: to listen for main ideas.**

● ▭ Make sure everyone understands what the listening passage is going to be about. Then play the tape and ask the students to listen and check the words in the vocabulary box as they hear them.

● Check the words they heard.

● Ask a student to tell the class through which main towns the route passed.

2. **Aim: to listen for specific information.**

● There is a great deal of specific information concerning journey time, distance, speed, and prices in the listening passage. Ask the students to try to remember which specific information they heard and underline it.

> **Answers**
> **Journey time:** 9 days
> **Distance:** 2,500 miles
> **Price of gas:** $1 a gallon
> **Speed limit:** 55 miles an hour
> **Price of motel rooms:** $20 to $35 per person

● You can ask the students to try to remember other numbers which the speaker mentions.

● ▭ Play the tape again and ask the students to check their answers.

● Ask the students if they would like to make a journey across the United States like Sarah's.

GRAMMAR

1. **Aim: to practice talking about journey time, distance, speed, and prices.**

● Ask the students to read the information about talking about journey time, distance, speed, and prices in the grammar box.

● Ask the students to check their answers to *Listening* activity 2. Encourage them to use the structures in the grammar box.

2. **Aim: to focus on asking questions about journey time, distance, speed, and prices.**

● Ask the students to think about places in their country which are:
– an hour away from each other by train, plane, car, or boat.
– 500 miles away from each other.
– half an hour away from each other by train, plane, car, or boat.
– 20 miles away from each other.
Ask them to write the questions.

● The students can then ask each other their questions. See if the answers correspond to what the questioners had in mind.

3. **Aim: to practice asking questions about journey time, distance, speed, and prices.**

● Write the following on the board: *speed limit in town, speed limit on freeways, price of a train ticket to the next big city, price of gas, price of a bus ticket in your town.* Ask the students to write questions saying how much these things cost or how fast you can go.

● Ask the students to work in pairs and ask and answer the questions.

SPEAKING

1. **Aim: to practice talking about journey time, distance, speed, and prices.**

● Ask the students to work in pairs and to talk about a memorable journey they have made. It doesn't need to be as significant as Sarah's journey across the southern United States. It could be a vacation journey or a memorable journey to work or school. Don't worry about correcting mistakes during this activity; this is an opportunity for fluency practice.

● Ask one or two students to describe their memorable journeys to the rest of the class.

2. **Aim: to practice using superlative adjectives; to ask questions about height, size, population, and temperature.**

● Ask the students to look at the information about America and to write two questions for each piece of information.

Answers	
What's the tallest building?	How tall is it?
What's the highest mountain?	How high is it?
What's the longest river?	How long is it?
What's the largest lake?	How large is it?
What's the biggest city?	How many people live there? *or* How big is it?
What's the hottest place?	How hot is it in the summer?
What's the coldest region?	How cold is it in the winter?

Metric Conversion
1,453 ft. = 443 m.
20,321 ft. = 6,194 m.
3,741 miles = 6,024 km.
122°F = 50°C
10°F = -12°C

3. **Aim: to practice talking about height, size, population, and temperature.**

● Ask the students to answer the questions they prepared in activity 2 with reference to their own country.

● If time is short, the students can write answers to the questions for homework.

Fluency 4

GENERAL COMMENTS

This lesson focuses on special occasions in private, public, religious, and national life, and the traditions and customs which accompany them. It also provides the opportunity to review the months of the year, ways of saying dates, and suitable expressions which are related to special occasions. You may like to point out that it isn't yet clear how we will pronounce the years in the twenty-first century, e.g. 2010 = two thousand and ten or twenty-ten.

VOCABULARY AND READING

1. Aim: to check students know the months of the year.
● Ask the students to put the months of the year in the right order.

Answers			
January	February	March	April
May	June	July	August
September	October	November	December

2. Aim: to check students know the days of the week.
● Ask the students to write down the days of the week.

Answer			
Sunday	Monday	Tuesday	Wednesday
Thursday	Friday	Saturday	

3. Aim: to practice speaking; to prepare for reading.
● Ask the students to talk about the associations they make with different days of the week. You may need to explain that in the Western world, Monday is traditionally the start of the week. Ask them if there are any days or months which have special associations for them.

4. Aim: to compare cultures; to practice reading for main ideas.
● This activity encourages the students to compare the associations of different days of the week in the United States with their own country. Ask them if there are any vocabulary difficulties, but before you explain the meaning of the word, find out if anyone else can explain it. You may also like to suggest that you'll only explain, say, eight words. This will encourage the students to choose these words carefully.

5. Aim: to practice speaking.
● Ask the students to talk about traditional activities associated with certain days of the week or months of the year in their country.

LISTENING AND SPEAKING

1. Aim: to prepare for listening; to practice reading for text organization.
● Ask the students to read the dialogue and to put it in the right order. You may like to point out that the tone of the speaker who is not celebrating his birthday is meant to be ironic.

Answer
D G H A I C B E F

2. Aim: to practice listening.
●  Play the tape and ask the students to listen and check their answers to 1.

3. Aim: to practice speaking.
● Ask the students to adapt the dialogue in 1 so it might be true for them. They can change any details they wish.

● Ask the students to act out the dialogue.

● Ask two or three pairs to act out the dialogue in front of the class.

FUNCTIONS

1. Aim: to focus on ordinal numbers.

● The students should have covered ordinal numbers in an earlier stage of their lessons, so this activity should be review. However, it is possible that for some students this is the first time they will have come across the form, in which case you may need to take more time over the activity.

● Ask the students to read the information in the functions box about saying dates and then to do the activity. You may like to ask them to do the activities in writing, or orally with the whole class.

Answers
eleventh twenty-third first fifteenth
second ninth thirty-first seventeenth

2. Aim: to practice saying dates.

● Once again, this activity should be review. If it is the first time the students have met dates, then take more time over it. You may need to supplement it with dates of your own.

Answers
1. January thirteenth, nineteen seventy-seven
2. April first, nineteen ninety-six
3. May third, nineteen eighty
4. Friday, January first, two thousand and ten
5. February sixth, nineteen ninety-nine
6. October twenty-fourth, two thousand and one.

3. Aim: to practice saying dates.

● The students require a little general knowledge to answer this question, but the information is fairly accessible. Here are the answers for the United States, except, of course for the last one.

Answers
December 25th; December 31st; January 1st;
October 31st; July 4th

4. Aim: to focus on appropriate greetings for special occasions.

● Ask the students to read the information in the functions box about saying the right thing and then to do this activity.

Answers
Merry Christmas; Happy New Year; Happy
Halloween; Happy birthday

5. Aim: to practice speaking; to practice saying dates.

● Ask the students to talk about other significant dates in the calendar.

LISTENING

1. Aim: to practice listening; to practice speaking.

● Make sure everyone understands that this is a jigsaw listening activity in which everyone listens to same tape but for different information. At this stage everyone is either working separately, or all the As are working together, all the Bs, and all the Cs etc.

● ▱ When everyone understands what they have to do, play the tape.

2. Aim: to practice speaking.

● At this stage everyone works in their original group, A, B, and C together. The chart represents a summary of what they've heard. Ask the students to work together and complete the chart.

● ▱ Play the tape again and ask the students to check the answers.

3. Aim: to practice speaking.

● Ask the students to choose important holidays in their country and to talk about the dates, the reason, and the customs.

● You may like to ask the students to write about the important date they chose for homework.

Progress Check 16–20

GENERAL COMMENTS

You can work through this Progress Check in the order shown, or concentrate on areas which may have caused difficulty in Lessons 16 to 20. You can also let the students choose the activities which they would like to or feel the need to do.

VOCABULARY

1. Aim: to focus on international words.
● Explain that many words in English are used in other languages too. Sometimes it's hard to know which language a word originally came from. Ask the students to group the words under the headings.

> **Answers**
> **food:** pizza, hamburger, sushi
> **sports:** football, tennis
> **places:** disco, restaurant, theater, stadium, museum
> **types of entertainment:** television, concert, movie, ballet, video
> **music:** disco, rock, opera, jazz

● Some words can go under other headings. Ask them to think of other words to go under the headings.

● Other possible groups of international words are science and technology and politics.

2. Aim: to focus on adjective suffixes.
● Ask the students to look back at Lesson 18 and write down the adjectives in the vocabulary box which end in -y, -ous, -ive, -ic, -ent, and -ful.

> **Answers**
> careful, confident, funny, imaginative, intelligent, lazy, nervous, optimistic, patient, pessimistic, sensitive, serious, tidy, thoughtful

3. Aim: to present or review male and female words.
● In Lesson 17 a difference was made between adjectives you usually use to describe men or women, but not both. Sentences 1 and 4 will be review, the rest may be new to the students.

> **Answer**
> 2 and 6 do not sound odd.

4. Aim: to present male and female words for clothes.

> **Answers**
> **Men:** underpants, shirt, boxers
> **Women:** skirt, bikini, bra, panties, nylons
> **Both:** boots, swimsuit, shorts, jacket, sandals, pyjamas

5. Aim: to help the students organize their vocabulary learning.
● Remind the students that they need to go back over their *Wordbanks* every so often. It also may be helpful to organize the words in different categories.

GRAMMAR

1. Aim: to review prepositions of time and place.

> **Answers**
> 1. The football season starts **in** August and finishes **in** January.
> 2. The ballet is **at** the Apollo Theater.
> 3. It's **on** Monday June 22 **at** 7:30 P.M.
> 4. The game is **at** 7:15 P.M. **on** Saturday.
> 5. The Olympics Games **in** 1996 were **in** Atlanta **in** the United States.
> 6. The movie starts **at** 3 P.M. **on** Saturday.

2. Aim: to review *to* and *at*.

> **Answers**
> 1. I like going **to** the theater.
> 2. I'm working **at** home tomorrow.
> 3. Let's meet **at** the movie theater.
> 4. The football game is **at** the main stadium.
> 5. Would you like to take us **to** the museum?
> 6. Let's walk **to** the swimming pool.

3. Aim: to review questions about people's appearance.

> **Answers**
> Who does he look like?
> How old is he?
> How tall is he?
> What color is his hair?
> What color are his eyes?
> What does he look like?

4. Aim: to review talking about personal appearance.

> **Answers**
> He looks like his father.
> He's 24 years old.
> He's six feet four inches tall.
> (You can say *He's six four* or *He's six foot four* or *He's six feet four inches tall*)
> He has blond hair.
> He has blue eyes.

5. **Aim:** to review talking about personal appearance.
- Ask the students to write their own sentences.

6. **Aim:** to review talking about personal appearance.

Answers
1. She's got a very **pleasant** face.
2. He's got no hair. He's completely **bald**.
3. He has a **long** gray beard.
4. She's over six foot. She's really **tall**.
5. He works as a model. He's very **good-looking**.
6. It's cold today. I'll wear a **coat**.

7. **Aim:** to review comparative/superlative adjectives.

Answers
big bigger biggest
calm calmer calmest
careful more careful most careful
confident more confident most confident
cute cuter cutest
friendly more friendly/friendlier most friendly/friendliest
generous more generous most generous
imaginative more imaginative most imaginative
informal more informal most informal
lazy lazier laziest
nervous more nervous most nervous
quiet quieter quietest
small smaller smallest
smart smarter smartest
thoughtful more thoughtful most thoughtful
tidy tidier tidiest
warm warmer warmest

8. **Aim:** to review comparative form of adjectives.

Answers
1. No, they aren't. They're more expensive.
2. No, he isn't. He's shorter than Phil.
3. No, it isn't. It's colder than Brazil.
4. No, it isn't. It's more difficult to buy nice clothes in the winter.
5. No, she isn't. She's older than Frank.
6. No, they aren't. They're more casual than South Americans.
7. No, he isn't. He's ruder than Jack.
8. No, he isn't. He's more hard-working than Joe.

9. **Aim:** to review superlative adjectives.

Answers
1. Yes, she's the kindest person I know.
2. Yes, it's the most beautiful town I know.
3. Yes, he's the politest person I know.
4. Yes, she's the shortest person I know.
5. Yes, it's the most expensive dress I know.
6. Yes, it's the most powerful car I know.
7. Yes, he's the most handsome man I know.
8 Yes, she's the most sensitive person I know.

10. **Aim:** to review talking about time, speed, distances, and prices.

Answers
A How **far** is it to the nearest gas station?
B It's fifty miles **away**.
A How **long** does it take **by** car?
B It's **a** five-minute drive.
A How long does it **take** to walk?
B It's thirty minutes **on** foot.
A How **much** is a ticket to Chicago?
B It **costs** $246.00.

SOUNDS

1. **Aim:** to focus on /ʊ/ and /uː/.
- Ask the students to say the words.
- ▭ Play the tape and ask the students to write the words in two columns.

Answers
/ʊ/: good book took cook
/uː/: blue shoe boot suit move

2. **Aim:** to focus on /dʒ/.
- ▭ Play each word and then pause the tape; ask the students to repeat each word.

Answers
geography journalist soldier engineer teenager job manager

3. **Aim:** to present simple transactional language for buying things.
- ▭ Ask the students to put the sentences in order.

Answers
c. Can I help you?
e. Yes, I'm looking for a sweater.
f. How about this one? It looks great on you.
d. It's too small. Do you have it in a bigger size?
b. Sorry. This is the largest size we have.
a. Well, thanks anyway.

- Remind the students that American people try to sound polite and friendly in most situations.

SPEAKING AND WRITING

Aim: to do a mutual dictation involving speaking and writing.
- The students are going to do a mutual dictation, in which they dictate to each other alternate lines of a short story. Ask them to turn to the Communication Activities and to follow the instructions.

- Ask the students to check their versions by showing each other the text in their Communication Activities.

Communication Activities

1. *Lesson 15*
Listening and Speaking, activity 2

Student A: 🔲 Listen and find out what Karen has for breakfast and what Pat has for lunch.

When the recording stops, turn back to page 39.

2. *Lesson 16*
Listening and Speaking, activity 1

Student A: 🔲 Listen and find out what type of entertainment karaoke is, and what type of music they play. Find out where they perform tango and the reasons why people enjoy it.

When the recording stops, turn back to page 44.

3. *Progress Check 16 - 20*
Speaking and Writing

Student B: Dictate these sentences to Student A in turn. Write down the sentences Student A dictates.

1. _____
   _____

2. So when a man finally got tickets he was surprised to find an empty seat between him and the next person, a woman dressed in black.

3. _____
   _____

4. The woman replied, "Yes, we bought them some months ago but then my husband died."

5. _____
   _____

6. The woman said, "Well, they're all at the funeral."

4. *Lesson 14*
Speaking, activity 2

Student A: Give *Student B* directions from places in column 1 to places in column 2. Tell *Student B* where you start from but not where you're going to.

1.	**2.**
Municipal Auditorium	French Market
Woldenburg Park	Jazz Meridien
Jackson Square	Louis Armstrong Park

Change around when you're ready.

5. *Lesson 11*
Reading, activity 3

Mostly "a"
You're extremely ambitious. You're never satisfied with your life and you're always trying to improve things. Try to relax and take things easy!

Mostly "b"
You're fairly ambitious. You are very aware that life has much to offer, but you don't feel you can achieve very much. Keep trying but don't make yourself unhappy.

Mostly "c"
You're so unambitious, you don't even know the meaning of the word. Look it up in a dictionary, if you can be bothered.

6. *Fluency 3*
Speaking and Listening 2, activity 2

Student A: 🔲 Listen and find out how much the following things cost:

Brazil: a gallon of milk, a meal in a restaurant, a new car, a house
Malaysia: a pound of fish, a bottle of wine, a newspaper, a gallon of gas

7. *Fluency 4*
Listening, activity 1

Student A: 🔲 Listen and find the answers to these questions:

1. What date is Valentine's Day and Labor Day?
2. What is the reason for Independence Day?
3. What customs are there on Mother's Day and Thanksgiving Day?

8. *Lesson 18*
Vocabulary, activity 2

The words you chose to describe the first person show the kind of person you'd like to be. The words you chose for the second person show how you think other people see you. The words you use to describe the third person show the real you, your true character!

9. *Progress Check 16 - 20*
Speaking and Writing

Student A: Dictate these sentences to *Student B* in turn. Write down the sentences *Student B* dictates.

1. *The Phantom of the Opera* was one of Broadway's most popular musicals and it was difficult to reserve seats.

2. _____

   _____

3. He said, "It took me a long time to get tickets for this show."

4. _____

   _____

5. The man said, "I'm so sorry. But why didn't you ask a friend or a relative to come with you?"

6. _____

   _____

10. *Fluency 4*
Listening, activity 1

Student B: 🔲 Listen and find the answers to these questions:

1. What date is Independence Day and Thanksgiving Day?

2. What is the reason for Valentine's Day and Mother's Day?

3. What customs are there on Labor Day?

11. *Lesson 16*
Listening and Speaking, activity 1

Student B: 🔲 Listen and find out where they perform karaoke and the reasons why people enjoy it. Find out who performs tango.

When the recording stops, turn back to page 44.

12. *Lesson 15*
Listening and Speaking, activity 2

Student C: 🔲 Listen and find out what Pat has for breakfast and what Karen has for dinner.

When the recording stops, turn back to page 39.

13. *Fluency 3*
Speaking and Listening 2, activity 2

Student B: 🔲 Listen and find out how much the following things cost:

Brazil: a pound of fish, a bottle of wine, a newspaper, a gallon of gas
Malaysia: a bus ticket, a movie ticket, a new television

14. *Progress Check 6 - 10*
Writing, activity 2

Read the passage and complete your version of the story

The Worst Baseball Team

On April 13, 1962, the City of New York welcomed its new baseball team, the New York Mets. Forty thousand people watched as the team paraded down Broadway and the band played "Hey, Look Me Over." The team rode in fourteen rainbow-colored cars. As they moved, they threw 10,000 plastic baseballs and bats into the crowd.

However, the team did not play very well. They lost their first nine games, which was almost a baseball record. At the end of the season, they had lost 120 games, which was more than any other team in the history of baseball!

Adapted from *Cannibals in the Cafeteria,*
by Stephen Pile

15. *Lesson 16*
Listening and Speaking, activity 1

Student C: [cassette] Listen and find out who performs karaoke. Find out what type of entertainment tango is and what type of music they play.

When the recording stops, turn back to page 44.

16. *Lesson 15*
Listening and Speaking, activity 2

Student B: [cassette] Listen and find out what Karen has for lunch and what Pat has for dinner.

When the recording stops, turn back to page 39.

17. *Lesson 14*
Speaking, activity 2

Student B: Give *Student A* directions from places in column 1 to places in column 2. Tell *Student A* where you start from but not where you're going to.

1.	2.
Palm Court Café	Aquarium of the Americas
Preservation Hall	World Trade Center
Jackson Brewery	Famous Door

Change around when you're ready.

18. *Fluency 3*
Speaking and Listening 2, activity 2

Student C: [cassette] Listen and find out how much the following things cost:

Brazil: a bus ticket, a movie ticket, a new television
Malaysia: a gallon of milk, a meal in a restaurant, a new car, a house

19. *Fluency 4*
Listening, activity 1

Student C: [cassette] Listen and find the answers to these questions:

1. What date is Mother's Day?
2. What is the reason for Thanksgiving Day and Labor Day?
3. What customs are there on Independence Day?

Grammar Review

CONTENTS

Present simple

Form

You use the contracted form in spoken and informal written English.

Be

Affirmative	Negative
I'm (I am)	I'm not (am not)
you	you
we 're (are)	we aren't (are not)
they	they
he	he
she 's (is)	she isn't (is not)
it	it

Questions	Short answers
Am I	Yes, I am.
	No, I'm not.
Are you/we/they?	Yes, you/we/they are.
	No, you/we/they're not.
Is he/she/it?	Yes, he/she/it is.
	No, he/she/it isn't.

Have

Affirmative	Negative
I	I
you have	you haven't (have not)
we	we
they	they
he	he
she has	she hasn't (has not)
it	it

Questions	Short answers
Have I/you/we/they?	Yes, I/you/we/they have.
	No, I/you/we/they haven't.
Has he/she/it?	Yes, he/she/it has.
	No, he/she/it hasn't.

Regular verbs

Affirmative	Negative
I	I
you work	you don't (do not) work
we	we
they	they
he	he
she works	she doesn't (does not) work
it	it

Questions	Short answers
Do I/you/we/they work?	Yes, I/you/we/they do.
	No, I/you/we/they don't.
Does he/she/it work?	Yes, he/she/it does.
	No, he/she/it doesn't.

Question words with *is/are*
What 's your name? Where are your parents?

Question words with *does/do*
What do you do? Where does he live?

Present simple: third person singular
(See Lesson 2.)

You add -*s* to most verbs.
takes, gets

You add -*es* to *do*, go, and verbs ending in -*ch*, -*ss*-, -*sh*, and -*x*.
goes, does, watches, finishes

You add -*ies* to verbs ending in -*y*.
carries, tries

Use

You use the present simple:

- to talk about customs and habits. (See Lesson 1.)
  In my country men go to restaurants on their own.

- to talk about routine activities. (See Lesson 2.)
  He gets up at 6:30.

- to talk about a habit. (See Lesson 5.)
  He smokes twenty cigarettes a day.

- to talk about a personal characteristic. (See Lesson 5.)
  She plays the piano.

- to talk about a general truth. (See Lesson 5.)
  You change money in a bank.

Present continuous

Form

You form the present continuous with *be* + present participle (-*ing*). You use the contracted form in spoken and informal written English.

Affirmative	Negative
I'm (am) working	I'm not (am not) working
you	you
we 're (are) working	we aren't (are not) working
they	they
he	he
she 's (is) working	she isn't (is not) working
it	it

Questions	Short answers
Am I working?	Yes, I am.
	No, I'm not.
Are you/we/they working?	Yes, you/we/they are.
	No, you/we/they aren't.
Is he/she/it working?	Yes, he/she/it is.
	No, he/she/it isn't.

Question words
What are you doing? Why are you laughing?

Present participle (-*ing*) endings

You form the present participle of most verbs by adding -*ing*.
go - going, visit – visiting

You add -*ing* to verbs ending in -*e*.
make- making, have- having

You double the final consonant of verbs of one syllable ending in a vowel and a consonant, and add -*ing*.
get- getting, shop- shopping

You add -*ing* to verbs ending in a vowel and -*y* or -*w*.
draw- drawing, play- playing

You don't usually use these verbs in the continuous form.
believe feel   hear , know   like   see   smell
sound   taste   think   understand   want

Use

You use the present continuous to say what is happening now or around now. There is an idea that the action or state is temporary. (See Lesson 5.)
It's raining. I'm learning English.

Past simple

Form
You use the contracted form in spoken and informal written English.

Be

Affirmative	Negative
I	I
he was	he wasn't (was not)
she	she
it	it
you	you
we were	we weren't (were not)
they	they

Have

Affirmative	Negative
I	I
you	you
we	we
they had	they didn't (did not) have
he	he
she	she
it	it

Regular verbs

Affirmative	Negative
I	I
you	you
we	we
they worked	they didn't work
he	he
she	she
it	it

Questions	Short answers
Did I/you/we/they work? he/she/it	Yes, I/you/we/they did. he/she/it
	No, I/you/we/they didn't. he/she/it

Question words
What did you do? Why did you leave?

Past simple endings

You add *-ed* to most regular verbs.
walk- walked, watch- watched

You add *-d* to verbs ending in *-e.*
close- closed, continue- continued

You double the consonant and add *-ed* to verbs ending in a vowel and a consonant.
stop- stopped, plan- planned

You drop the *-y* and add *-ied* to verbs ending in *-y.*
study- studied, try- tried

You add —*ed* to verbs ending in a vowel + *-y.*
play- played, annoy- annoyed

Pronunciation of past simple endings

/t/ *finished, liked, walked*
/d/ *continued, lived, stayed*
/ɪd/ *decided, started, visited*

Expressions of past time
(See Lesson 8.)

yesterday	*the day before yesterday*	*last weekend*
last night	*last month*	*last year*

Use
You use the past simple:

● to talk about a past action or event that is finished.
(See Lessons 6, 7, and 8.)
He shipped it over from the River Thames.

Future simple (*will*)

Form

You form the future simple with *will* + infinitive. You use the contracted form in spoken and informal written English.

Affirmative	Negative
I	I
you	you
we	we
they 'll (will) work	they won't (will not) work
he	he
she	she
it	it

Questions	Short answers
Will I/you/we/they work? he/she/it/	Yes, I/you/we/they will. he/she/it/
	No, I/you/we/they won't. he/she/it/

Question words

What will you do? Where will you go?

Expressions of future time

tomorrow   tomorrow morning   tomorrow afternoon   next week   next month   next year   in two days   in three months   in five years

Use

You use the future simple:

- to make a prediction or express an opinion about the future. (See Lesson 12.)
  I think most people will need English for their jobs.

- to talk about decisions you make at the moment of speaking. (See Lesson 13.)
  I'll give you the money right now.

- to talk about things you are not sure will happen with *probably* and *perhaps*. (See Lesson 13.)
  He'll probably spend three weeks there. Perhaps he'll stay two days in Rio.

- to offer to do something. (See Lesson 13.)
  OK, I'll buy some food.

Verb patterns

There are several possible patterns after certain verbs which involve -*ing* form verbs and infinitive constructions with or without *to*.

-*ing* form verbs

You can put an -*ing* form verb after certain verbs. (See Lesson 4.)
I love walking. She likes swimming. They hate lying on the beach.

Remember that *would like to do something* refers to an activity at a specific time in the future.
I'd like to go to the movies next Saturday.

Try not to confuse it with *like doing something* which refers to an activity you enjoy all the time.
I like going to the movies. I go most weekends.

To + infinitive

You can put *to* + infinitive after many verbs. Here are some of them:

*agree   decide   go   have   hope   earn   leave
like   need   offer   start   try   want*

Use

You use *to* + infinitive with *(be) going to* and *would like to*. (See below.)

Have to

You use *have to* and *have got to* to talk about something you're obliged or strongly advised to do:
You have to wear a helmet.

In negatives, you use *don't have to*:
You don't have to go to work on Sunday.
Don't have to means that something is not necessary.

Going to

You use *(be) going to*:
- to talk about future intentions or plans. (See Lesson 11.)
  I'm going to be a doctor. (I'm studying medicine.)
- to talk about things which are arranged and sure to happen with *(be) going to*. (See Lesson 13.)
  I'm going to visit South America. I've bought my ticket.

You often use the present continuous and not *going to* with *come* and *go*.
Are you coming tonight?
NOT ~~Are you going to come tonight?~~
He's going to South America.
NOT ~~He's going to go to South America.~~

Would like to

You use *would like to*:

- to talk about ambitions, hopes, or preferences.
  (See Lesson 11.)
  I'd like to speak English fluently.

Have (got)

Form

You use the contracted form in spoken and informal written English.

Affirmative	Negative
I	I
you 've (have) got	you haven't (have not) got
we	we
they	they
he	he
she 's (has) got	she hasn't (has not) got
it	it

Questions	Short answers
Have I/you/we/they got?	Yes, I/you/we/they have.
	No, I/you/we/they haven't.
Has he/she/it got?	Yes, he/she/it has.
	No, he/she/it hasn't.

Use

You use *have (got)* to talk about facilities, possession, or relationship. (See Lesson 10.)
I've got a new car. or *I have a new car.*

You don't use *have got* to talk about a habit or routine.
I often have lunch out. NOT I often have got lunch out.

You don't usually use *have got* in the past. You use the past simple of *have*.
I had a headache yesterday. NOT I had got a headache.

Questions

You can form questions in two ways:

- with a question word such as *who, what, which, where, how, why*.
  What's your name?

- without a question word.
  Are you American?

You can put a noun after *what* and *which*. (See Lesson 1.)
What time is it? Which road will you take?

You often say *what* to give the idea that there is more choice.
What books have you read lately?

You can put an adjective or an adverb after *how*.
(See Lessons 15 and 20.)
How much is it? How long does it take by car? How fast can you drive?

You can use *who, what,* or *which* as pronouns to ask about the subject of the sentence. You don't use *do* or *did*.
(See Lessons 1 and 7.)
What's your first name?
Who invented the first traveler's check?

You can use *who, what,* or *which* and other question words to ask about the object of the sentence. You use *do* or *did*.
(See Lessons 1 and 7.)
What did he call his invention?

Articles

You can find the main uses of articles in Lesson 3. Here are some extra details.

You use *an* for nouns which begin with a vowel.
an armchair

You use *one* if you want to emphasise the number.
One hundred and twenty-two.

Before vowels you pronounce *the* /ði:/.

You do not use the definite article with parts of the body. You use a possessive adjective.
I'm washing my hair.

Plurals

You can find the main rules for forming plurals in Lesson 3.

Possessives

You can find the main uses of the possessive *'s* in Lesson 9.
You can find a list of possessive adjectives in Lesson 9.

Expressions of quantity

Countable and uncountable nouns

Countable nouns have both a singular and a plural form.
(See Lesson 15.)
an apple – some apples, a melon – some melons,
a potato – some potatoes, a cup – (not) many cups,
a cookie – a few cookies

Uncountable nouns do not usually have a plural form.
some wine, some cheese, some fruit, (not) much meat, a little coffee

If you talk about different kinds of uncountable nouns they become countable.
Beaujolais and Bordeaux are both French wines.

Expressions with countable or uncountable nouns

You can put countable or uncountable nouns with these expressions of quantity.

lots of apples, lots of cheese, hardly any apples, hardly any cheese, a lot of fruit, a lot of potatoes.

Some and any
(See Lesson 15.)

Affirmative	*There's some milk in the refrigerator.*
	There are some apples on the table.
Negative	*I haven't got any brothers.*
	There isn't any cheese.

Questions

You usually use *any* for questions.
Is there any sugar?

You can use *some* in questions when you are making an offer or a request, and you expect the answer to be *yes*.
Would you like some coffee?
Can I have some sugar, please?

Much and many

You use *many* with countable nouns and *much* with uncountable nouns. (See Lesson 15.)
How many eggs would you like?
How much butter do you need?

Too much/many, not enough, fewer, less, and more

You can put a countable noun in the plural after *too many*, *not enough*, and *fewer*.
There are too many people.
There aren't enough clean rivers.
In the United States there are fewer men than women.

You can put an uncountable noun after *too much*, *not enough*, *more*, and *less*.
There's too much noise. There isn't enough farmland.
There's more pollution.

You can put an adjective after *too* or between *not* and *enough*.
The sea is too polluted. The air isn't clean enough.

Making comparisons

Comparative and superlative adjectives

Form

You add *-er* to most adjectives for the comparative form, and *-est* for the superlative form. (See Lesson 18.)
cold colder coldest   cheap cheaper cheapest

You add *-r* to adjectives ending in *-e* for the comparative form and *-st* for the superlative form.
large larger largest   fine finer finest

You add *-ier* to adjectives ending in *-y* for the comparative form, and *-iest* for the superlative form.

happy happier happiest
friendly friendlier friendliest

You double the last letter of adjectives ending in *-g*, *-t*, or *-n*.
hot hotter hottest
thin thinner thinnest

You use *more* for the comparative form and *most* for the superlative form of longer adjectives.
expensive more expensive most expensive
important more important most important

Some adjectives have irregular comparative and superlative forms.
good better best bad worse worst

More than, less than, as … as

- You put *than* before the object of comparison. (See Lesson 19.)
  Children wear more casual clothes than their parents.

- You use *less … than* to change the focus of the comparison.
  Parents wear less casual clothes than their children.

- You can put *much* before the comparative adjective, *more*, or *less* to emphasize it.
  They're much less formal than they were.

- You use *as … as* to show something is the same.
  They're as casual as teenagers all over the world.

- You use not *as … as* to show something is different.
  Dresses are not as popular as in Western countries.

So, because

- You can join two sentences with *so* to describe a consequence.
  She often took the plane so she didn't look at the safety instructions.
- You can join the same two sentences with *because* to describe a reason.
  She didn't look at the safety instructions because she often took the plane.

Prepositions of place

(See Lesson 14.)

Prepositions of time and place: *in, at, on, to*

(See Lesson 16.)

Use

You use *in*:

- with times of the day: *in the morning, in the afternoon.*
- with months of the year: *in March, in September*
- with years: *in 1996, in 1872*
- with places: *in New York, in Mexico City, in the bank*

You use *at*:

- with times of the day: *at night, at seven o'clock*
- with places: *at the theater, at the stadium*

You use *on*:

- with days, dates: *on Friday, on July 15th*

You use *to*:

- with places: *Let's go to Seattle.*

Adverbs of frequency

Use

You use an adverb of frequency to say how often things happen. (See Lesson 1.)

They always take their shoes off.
We usually take wine or flowers.
We often wear jeans and sweaters.
We sometimes arrive about fifteen minutes after.
We never ask personal questions.

Tapescripts

Lesson 1 Speaking and Listening, activity 2

Situation 1

PAT Yumio! Great to see you. You look great!

YUMIO How are you, Pat?

PAT We're all fine. Come in, come in.

YUMIO Pat, this is my friend Rosario Rodriguez.

PAT Hello, Rosario, how do you do? I'm very pleased to meet you.

ROSARIO How do you do?

PAT Come in. We're in the back room, come on through. Now, when was the last time we got together?

Situation 2

WOMAN Excuse me!

WAITER Yes, can I help you?

WOMAN Yes, I'd like a Coke, please.

WAITER Sure. Small, medium, or large?

WOMAN Sorry, I don't understand.

WAITER What size? Would you like a big, small, or a medium Coke?

WOMAN Oh, small, please.

WAITER Here you go.

WOMAN Thank you. How much is it?

WAITER Ninety cents.

Lesson 1 Speaking and Listening, activity 3

1. What's your first name?
2. Where do you live?
3. Are you married?
4. What do you do?
5. Do you have any brothers and sisters?
6. Where do you come from?

Lesson 2 Listening, activity 1

Speaker 1

JO-ANN I get up around seven o'clock and have breakfast. Then I have to leave home at about eight, I guess. It takes me about forty minutes to ride the bus downtown and start work at about nine.

Q Do you like your job?

JO-ANN It's OK. Some days it's fine, some days you get some real tricky customers.

Q Do you get time off for lunch?

JO-ANN Sure, I stop around twelve-thirty and then at one o'clock I take a walk in the park—just to get some fresh air, you know. If the weather's OK, I'll have a sandwich or something there.

Q Mmm. Does it get busy in the afternoon?

JO-ANN No more than in the morning, I guess. When the bank's open, people call at all times.

Q So when do you leave work?

JO-ANN I leave work at about five in the evening, and sometimes I take the bus back home. Other times I go to a bar or a coffee shop with my friends. I guess I usually go to bed around eleven-thirty.

Speaker 2

GEORGE I get up very early these days, much earlier than when I was at work, at about six o'clock, I guess.

Q Why so early?

GEORGE Oh, I like to see the sun rise, have a walk on the beach, you know. If it's hot, I go for a swim in the sea before breakfast.

Q And what time do you have breakfast?

GEORGE I get breakfast ready for about eight-fifteen and take it up to Hilary who's still in bed. Then we go shopping in the local mall, meet some friends, have lunch, that sort of thing.

Q What time do you have lunch, then?

GEORGE At about half-past twelve, I guess. And in the afternoon, I go for another walk, maybe play a little golf, have a swim, go down to the community center to join Hilary.

Q And what about in the evening?

GEORGE Well, I meet my friends at about five-thirty and have a drink or two at the golf club. We talk for about an hour or so, then I go home for dinner at seven o'clock. Maybe we have friends around, maybe we go for dinner, it just depends. But most nights we're in bed by ten-thirty. It's a great life!

Lesson 5 Listening and Vocabulary, activity 2

Conversation 1

WOMAN Good morning.

TELLER Good morning. How may I help you?

WOMAN I'd like three hundred dollars worth of Italian lira, please.

TELLER Traveler's checks or cash?

WOMAN Traveler's checks.

TELLER Could I have your passport, please? Thank you. Would you sign and date them, please?

WOMAN Here you are.

TELLER That makes four hundred and twenty-one thousand lira.

WOMAN Thank you.

TELLER Thank you. Have a nice trip.

Conversation 2

WAITRESS Good evening, sir. A table for two?

MAN Yes, but could we sit by the window, please?

WAITRESS Certainly sir. Come this way. Here you are sir, ma'am. Can I take your coats?

WOMAN Thank you.

WAITRESS My name is Lori, and I'll be your server tonight. Can I get you a drink while you look at the menu?

MAN Not for me, thank you.

WOMAN No, thanks. I think we'll just have some wine with the meal, please.

WAITRESS I recommend the lamb this evening. It's cooked with spices, it's a Lebanese dish, specialty of the chef. I'm sure you'll like it. It comes with mixed vegetables.

MAN Sounds great!

WOMAN Well, I'd like to have a look at the menu anyway.

WAITRESS Certainly, ma'am. I'll come back when you're ready to order.

Conversation 3

WOMAN Hi. I need a round trip ticket to San Diego, leaving tomorrow.

TRAVEL AGENT Will you be spending the weekend in San Diego?

WOMAN Yes. I'm coming back on Tuesday—the 12th.

TRAVEL AGENT OK. Uh, that's going to be $279 plus tax. Are you a "Miles Plus" member?

WOMAN I don't think so. What is it?

TRAVEL AGENT Well, the airline keeps track of all the miles you fly with them, and when you reach 25,000 miles, you get a free round trip ticket to any destination in the U.S.

WOMAN Sounds great! Sign me up!

Conversation 4

MAN What would you recommend for a cough?

PHARMACIST Well, I can give you some cough medicine, but if it's very bad, you ought to see a doctor.

MAN No, it's not too bad. I thought I'd try something over the counter first.

PHARMACIST Have you got a headache and a fever?

MAN Yes.

PHARMACIST Well, try this medicine for your cough and these tablets for the headache and fever. They're a kind of aspirin which you dissolve in hot water.

MAN Thank you. How much is that?

PHARMACIST That'll be eight dollars and fifty cents, please.

MAN Thank you.

Fluency 1 **Listening and Reading, activity 3**

KELLY Hello, Joe. How are you?

JOE Hi, Kelly. Fine, thanks. Hey, you look great today! That's a beautiful dress.

KELLY Thanks. How was your weekend?

JOE OK.

TEACHER Good morning, everyone. Uh, my name is Steve Smith. You can call me Steve. How are you all today?

JOE Hi, Steve! We're all fine.

KELLY Good morning, Mr. Smith.

TEACHER Please sit down, everyone.

DAVE Oh, I'm sorry I'm late.

TEACHER No problem, we've just started. Now, take out your textbooks and turn to page 15.

JOE Can I ask a question? Can you tell me what *Buenos dias* means?

TEACHER It means *good day* or *hello* in Spanish. OK, I'd like you to work in pairs.

DAVE Is it OK if I work with you, Kelly?

KELLY Yes, of course.

Fluency 1 **Functions, activity 4**

A B C D E F G H I J K L M N O P Q R S T U V W X Y Z

Fluency 1 **Functions, activity 5**

A H J K
B C D E G P T V Z
F L M N S X
I Y
O
Q U W
R

Fluency 1 **Reading and Listening, activity 2**

Q OK, Jennifer. Now you're taking a Spanish course, aren't you?

JENNIFER Yeah, I am.

Q Is it all right if I ask you a few questions about what you do in the classroom, classroom behavior, that kind of thing?

JENNIFER Sure.

Q OK, my first question is: Do you greet people when you come into class and if so, what do you say?

JENNIFER You mean do I greet my fellow students or do I greet the teacher?

Q Well, I guess both.

JENNIFER Well, yeah, I greet my fellow students. I probably say "Hi, how are you doing?" and like if I know their names, "Hi, Bill, what's up?" or something like that. To the teacher I guess I usually say "Good evening."

Q And do you stand up when your teacher comes into class?

JENNIFER Stand up? No, we don't usually do that.

Q What do you call your teacher?

JENNIFER Uh well, at the beginning of the year when we didn't know her so well we called her Ms. Sanchez. But now we usually call her Maria.

Q I see. So now you know her better you use her first name.

JENNIFER Yeah. We call her Maria.

Q Right. And if you're late for class, do you say anything? Do you say you're sorry you're late?

JENNIFER Uh, yes, of course. I mean I would always apologise for being late. I'd say something like "I'm sorry I'm late."

Q OK. Next question. Who do you think should talk most in a language class, the teacher or the students?

JENNIFER Oh boy, that's a hard one. Well, I guess ideally the students should talk most because that means they're practicing the language. But I think at the beginning of our course Maria, the teacher, talked most. But I guess now that we've gotten a bit better at Spanish, it's really the students who talk most. It's a great class, we're all really enthusiastic and we want to learn, so we talk.

Q Well, that's great. But do you only speak when you're spoken to?

JENNIFER No, no, I mean if we're asked a question, yeah, we speak, but you know a lot of times we ask questions and we might have an idea, you know, something to say on a subject and then, well, no, we wouldn't wait to be spoken to, I mean to be asked, we would go right ahead and say what we wanted to say.

Q Are you expected to work with other students?

JENNIFER Work with other students? How do you mean?

Q Well, I guess, work in pairs, do an exercise together.

JENNIFER Oh, yeah, I mean we do a lot of our practice in pairs and in groups. And when we're doing an exercise we help each other.

Q So do you think it's OK to cheat sometimes?

JENNIFER Cheat? Uh uh. I mean, that depends what you mean. I don't think it's OK to cheat in a test, you know, I mean, when you're supposed to be working on your own and your score on the test is being used to assess your progress. No. But exercises in class, I mean homework perhaps, I mean then I think it's OK to help each other—I don't know if that counts as cheating!

Q Oh, OK. Now in class, you've already said that you ask questions.

JENNIFER Yeah, of course.

Q Right, but do you ask them during the class or do you wait until the end?

JENNIFER Oh, definitely usually during the class.

Q And in your language lessons, which of these things would you expect? I've got a list here—can you take a look at this list?

JENNIFER Sure. All right, let me see... quizzes, um yeah sometimes; exams, yeah maybe at the end of the course. Dictionaries, oh, definitely, we use them a lot. Other reference books? No, not usually. Exercises, songs and role plays: yeah, we do a lot of those. Yeah, I mean in fact looking at this list, I would say we have all of these things, except perhaps field trips.

Q Which of these things do you expect in lessons on other subjects?

JENNIFER Um, well, that's kind of hard to say as I don't take any other classes. Sorry, I can't help you there!

Q Never mind. OK, tell me how do you know when a class is over?

JENNIFER Well, there's no bell or anything like that to say that time's up. Uh, I guess the teacher usually tells us. She'll say something like, you know, "OK, that's it for this week, now for homework can you do this or that", you know, something like that.

Q And do you wait for the teacher to leave before you leave?

JENNIFER Oh, no, we don't do that. I mean, some students leave straight away and some wait behind to talk to each other or, you know, to the teacher. It's not a very formal class.

Q It sounds like fun. OK, Jennifer, thanks for your help.

JENNIFER You're welcome.

Lesson 8 **Listening and Speaking, activity 2**

I arrived in this town quite late, about ten o'clock, I guess, and looked for somewhere to stay. I didn't have a reservation anywhere, because I didn't expect to stay there. The main hotel was full, but the concierge told me there was a small motel down the road. I left the car where it was and I went down the road and actually I walked right past the motel, because I saw there were no lights on. I knocked on the door—there was no bell, or anything—and a man opened the door. He was unshaven and wearing a very dirty T-shirt, and the television was on. I asked if he had a room and without saying a word, he picked up a key from behind the desk and pushed a registration card at me. I wrote my name, but not my address, I don't know why, I felt there was something wrong. I saw that all the keys were on their hooks, so either all the other guests were out or I was the only person staying there. I followed him along a dimly-lit passage—most of the light bulbs had burned out—and he showed me a very dusty room. He gave me the key and closed the door. I sat down on the tiny single bed and wondered what to do. It was a horrible room with a sink, but no shower or toilet or anything. I decided I wanted to check out right away but I was frightened by the man in the office. I ran out of my room and walked quickly past his office, but he didn't look up. I quickly said, "I've left my suitcase in my car", and ran off, up the street, and locked myself in the car—I was so scared. I slept in the car that night!

Lesson 9 **Vocabulary and Listening, activity 2**

I've got a big family, actually. My grandmother lives with my mother and father, and her name is Pat. Then I have a brother whose name is Ray, who lives in Rochester, and a sister, Kelly, who lives in Syracuse. My aunt's name is Christine and my uncle's name is Tony. Then, of course, there's my husband Larry. His family comes from Buffalo, and that's where we live now. Oh, I nearly forgot, my mother's name is Carol and my father's, Craig. We're very close.

Lesson 10 **Vocabulary and Listening, activity 2**

Q What's it like living in Taipei?
LAURA Oh, I love it! The people are so friendly and helpful, and it's big, but not too big, you know?
Q What's the population?
LAURA About three and a half million, I think... I'm not sure. But it doesn't feel really congested, like a lot of other big cities. It's fairly polluted, I guess... nothing like L.A., though! And it's got everything... parks, museums... fantastic museums!... restaurants to die for...
Q Is it very industrialized?
LAURA Oh, sure... out in the suburbs there are, you know, the factories and the industrial estates, and... uh... the city center is pretty modern. But there is still a lot of the "old" Taipei... like Wanhua, which has houses and shops and temples and family shrines that are all about 100 years old. I go down there a lot to take photos and just watch people.
Q What are the people like?
LAURA Oh, really friendly and helpful... I'm taking Chinese classes at the university now, but when I first arrived I was totally lost, and people kept helping me out... taking me places, and translating for me...
Q Wow! Uh... is Taipei expensive?
LAURA Well, it's getting that way, but I guess I get paid pretty well, so it doesn't seem... I mean, clothes and food are really cheap. But I pay about twice as much rent as I would in the U.S., and my apartment is, well, tiny!

Lesson 10 **Vocabulary and Listening, activity 5**

SPEAKER 1 It's quite cheap to live here, although in certain parts of town houses are really very expensive. Everyday things in the stores are very cheap compared with the U.S., although clothes can cost a lot.
SPEAKER 2 Oh, it's incredible, I mean, there are so many cars and trucks. You see, the railroad system is not very extensive so everything has to go by road. But at rush hour in the center of town, it's so busy.
SPEAKER 3 It's a very interesting place to visit, although I wouldn't call the buildings beautiful. But the palace is quite fascinating and well worth spending a day on. And then there are some wonderful churches and mosques.
SPEAKER 4 It's really small, about one hundred thousand people, and the city center is really very compact, although the suburbs stretch for about five miles in each direction.
SPEAKER 5 It rains all the time, it's famous for that. Even in the middle of the summer you are never certain that the sun will shine all day, so it's difficult to make plans for any outdoor activities.
SPEAKER 6 Well, you can still walk the streets at night and not feel nervous that someone's going to attack you. But I think it's a good idea to be sensible and keep your money and valuables safe in your jacket. You never know, it can happen anywhere, can't it?

Fluency 2 **Listening and Speaking, activity 2**

1.
JERRY What are you doing this evening?
KATE Not much.
JERRY Would you like to go to a movie?
KATE Sure. What's on?
JERRY There's a new Quentin Tarantino movie that just came out...
KATE Great! What time does it start?
JERRY Seven o'clock. Why don't we leave here at a quarter after six?
KATE Make it six o'clock. The traffic is pretty bad at that time.
JERRY Six o'clock, then. See you downstairs.
KATE OK. See you later .

2.
LENNY What time does the plane leave?
DIANA Ten thirty.
LENNY And what time is it now?
DIANA It's about nine fifteen.
LENNY How long does it take to get to the airport?
DIANA About half an hour.
LENNY Well, we ought to leave right away, I guess. I don't want to miss it.
DIANA Relax! We've got plenty of time.

Fluency 2 **Listening and Speaking, activity 6**

BILL OK. I've been asked to talk a little about daily routines in the U.S. and the times people do things. First I'd have to say that this is a huge country and it's very difficult to say what is typical. I mean, everybody's different. But I'll give it a try.

Getting up in the morning. Well this kind of depends on your job. I mean, yeah, I guess a lot of people do get up at about 7 o'clock. Probably most people, yeah.

As for starting work, well, again that depends on what you do, but, yes, working hours in the U.S. are generally considered to be nine to five, so I guess it's OK to say that people generally start work at nine o'clock.

There's usually a coffee break at eleven o'clock. Um. No, I'd have to say that's wrong. People drink coffee all the time. I don't think there's a specific time, a specific break when they drink coffee. No.

You have to be on time for appointments. Yeah, you do. Business appointments that is. You're expected to be on time for business appointments. It's kind of different for friends, though. As long as you're not too late. I think it's OK to be late for a meeting with a friend: maybe ten to fifteen minutes or so.

Lunch can be anytime from noon. I wouldn't say that everyone eats lunch exactly at noon. No, I'd say that's wrong. I mean, in a lot of companies lunch is from 1 to 2, so, no, I don't think it's true to say that lunch is *usually* at noon. Though it often is.

In the U.S. it's not common to spend time with co-workers after work. We usually like to get back home to our families after work.

Dinner *can* be at eight o'clock but again, I don't think you can say it's *usually* at eight. Like lunch, different people eat at different times. I'd say that if you're invited to friends for dinner that *is* usually at eight, but with your family, well, you might eat a lot earlier than that, especially if you've got young kids.

Most people *are* in bed before midnight. I guess that's probably true, but there are a lot of people who like to party all night! They aren't *most* people though. I guess if you're talking about *most* people, then, yeah, in bed before midnight is about right.

Fluency 2 **Functions, activity 3**

1.

A OK. Here's your boarding pass. Boarding time will be ten thirty from gate 38.
B Thank you.

2.
MOTHER Come on, John. Finish your cereal quickly or you'll miss the bus. Come on, it's ten after eight.
JOHN Oh, Mom, do I have to go to school today?
MOTHER Yes, you do!

3.

This is Cooper and Ramirez. We are sorry that there's no one here to take your call. The office will be open again tomorrow at eight thirty A.M. If you would like to leave a message, please speak after the tone.

4.

A Excuse me, can you tell me what track the nine-fifteen to Boston leaves from?
B Track 10, sir.

Lesson 12 **Listening, activity 2**

Q Maggie, um… I'd like to ask you first, um… at what age do people start learning English these days?
MAGGIE Um… well, in many countries children start learning English when they go to school, but I think in some countries they're starting to teach English to much younger children and I think this will become more and more common around the world.
GREG Yeah, that's right 'cause I know that um… in some countries they're even having English lessons for six-year-old children so, they'll certainly be learning as soon as they start school, if not before.
Q I see. And do you think, um… English will soon be the universal language?
MAGGIE Oh, I think most adults already speak some English, um… even if it's only a word or two here and there, because, well, English is very common and very useful.
GREG Mmm… I…
Q What about you, Greg?
GREG Well, I think Maggie's absolutely right. Because, if you think about it, already there are so many words, for example to do with computers, um, you know, that are in English and that are used internationally, for example, um… "radio, television, hamburger," these are all international words—English words though. So I think pretty soon there'll be very few people who don't speak English, not just a few words but, you know, really communicating in it.
Q And do you think, Maggie, that teachers will start using English to teach other subjects, you know, for instance, geography or science, and that it'll be used in schools all over the world?
MAGGIE Yes, I sure do. I think that teachers will start experimenting with that. I think in many ways it's the best way to learn English.
GREG Mmm…
Q Greg?
GREG Um… I'm not so sure. I think some classes will be in English for

sure, um… for example, science. But I think most others won't be in English. There's no reason why every single subject should be taught in English.
Q Right. Now, what about North American life, culture, and institutions, do you think that it's important to know about those?
MAGGIE No, not at all. I mean, I don't think that English as a language has anything to do with, like, mom's apple pie and the American Dream. I mean, it's an international language and, um… it can be used for communication between people who don't know each other's language, um… as a tool really. So, I don't think that the cultural roots of English are important at all.
GREG Well, I disagree, because I think you have to understand, er… the culture of a country, just because there are some words that mean different things to different people depending on what country they're in, for example… the word "family" … it means one thing to North Americans and another to South Americans. Uh… the word "police" means different things to different people. You always have to know something about the background and the culture of a country before you can fully understand the language.
Q Mmm. What about in the workplace? How important is English there, what's its role?
MAGGIE Well, I think it's really important and I think more and more people will use it at work—it's, it's… easily understood wherever you come from and I think, well, actually, everyone will need to use more English for their work.
Q Greg?
GREG Um… I think some people will need to use more English, particularly people working in big companies who have to travel a lot and do a lot of business between different countries, but I think for the majority of the population in any country, uh, you know, who don't… who aren't involved in international business or moving around or traveling, then I think they'll continue to do business in their own language.
Q And the traditional language class as we know it—do you think that that will continue or will there be other forms of teaching, such as, you know, teaching involving television and computers, and so forth?
MAGGIE Well, I think that the traditional language class will still exist. Um… I think that personal contact is very important with the language teacher and, um… of course, there is more than one person in a class, you can interact with the other students and I think that that's much more valuable than just staring at a computer screen or, you know, listening to cassettes.
Q Mmm. Do you agree with that, Greg?
GREG Not entirely. We live in a computer age now, and I think that computers and other … videos for example—all those interactive programs that you use with videos—will allow people to learn foreign languages in a different way on their own, so that you don't have to depend on teachers and other students. I'm not sure, but I think that's how it'll be.
Q And finally, Maggie, do you think that English will ever become more important than the language of the native speaker?
MAGGIE Well, no. I think obviously English is important, but I think your own language and your own culture and traditions are more important to you and I think it's good to respect those and to hold on to them.
GREG Yes, I agree. I think it would be very arrogant to think that English would be more important than your own language, I mean, 'cause your language is part of your culture and your personal identity and your national identity, isn't it?
MAGGIE Mmm. I think so.
Q Thank you very much.
GREG No problem!

Lesson 13 **Listening, activity 2**

CATHY So, what are you going to do this summer?
RYAN I'm going to South America.
CATHY Great!
RYAN I'm going to be traveling around a lot and I'll probably spend three weeks there.
CATHY So, where are you going?
RYAN To start out, I'm going to fly to Rio and maybe I'll stay there for a couple of days.
CATHY Do you know anyone there?
RYAN No, but I've always wanted to go to Rio. It's supposed to be totally awesome. And I'll probably go up the Sugar Loaf mountain, in the cable car, like all the tourists.
CATHY And where are you going after that?
RYAN I'm going to fly to Santiago in Chile, where I've got some friends. We'll probably spend some time doing some sightseeing and then we're going to lie on the beach for a few days in Valparaiso, which is on the coast, not far away from Santiago. Then I'm flying to Lima where I'm going to meet my girlfriend and then we're going to visit Machu Picchu in the mountains.
CATHY And visit the ruins? Oh, fantastic!
RYAN Yeah, it should be pretty cool. And then we'll probably go somewhere on the Amazon. I don't know where yet, but I'd like to spend a week in the jungle. Then we'll probably fly home.
CATHY Well, have a great time!

Lesson 13 **Listening, Activity 4**

CATHY Do you have a good guide book?
RYAN No, I don't. But I'm going to get one. It's on my list of things to buy before I go.
CATHY Well, they say the best one is "South American Handbook."
RYAN Really? Well, I'll get it when I go downtown.
CATHY Look, I'm going downtown right now because I need to do some shopping. I'll buy it for you at the bookstore, if you want.
RYAN Really?
CATHY Yeah, sure.
RYAN Well, I'll give you the money for it right now.
CATHY OK, and I'll bring it to your place tonight. Who knows, maybe I'll borrow it from you someday.
RYAN OK. Thanks a lot.

Lesson 15 **Grammar, activity 2**

A We need some water. How many bottles do we need?
B Two. And we don't have any fruit. Do you want to get some peaches?
A OK. Do we have any coffee?
B No, how much do we need?
A Just one pound.

Lesson 15 **Listening and Speaking, activity 2**

Q So, Pat, you've lived in the United States for five years. Where do you live?
PAT In San Francisco.
Q Uh-huh. And, um… we were wondering what typical meals were like for you. I mean, what do you have for a typical breakfast?
PAT Well, a lot of people eat a lot—you know, steak, eggs, hash browns, and so forth… but I can't eat that much. I have coffee, and I like cereal, so, I'll eat grape nuts or granola, something like that. But, usually I just have, um… fruit and… juicing is very big now, of course.
Q Uh-huh.
PAT I'll juice a lot of fruit in a blender.
Q Is there any fruit that's especially good?
PAT Um… apricots are very good. Apricots, oranges, bananas.
Q And, when you juice things, you make a mixture of these fruits, do you?
PAT Yes, I basically just throw everything in, and, um, juice it and then drink and then that keeps me going for most of the morning.
Q Hmm. How about lunch? Do you have lunch?

PAT Well, if I'm going to eat lunch, I tend to go more for, um… either light pasta dishes, or vegetable platter where you have, you know, beans, courgettes, aubergines, that sort of thing.
Q Courgettes?
PAT Oh, I mean zucchini!
Q And aubergines are…?
PAT That's eggplant.
Q Aubergine, right!
PAT Old habits die hard! But, um… more often than not, probably just a sub sandwich. Full of meat…
Q And is that your main meal?
PAT No, no, no. The main meal is in the evening.
Q And what do you have then?
PAT Um… well, San Francisco is… you can eat very well, um… if you go to seafood restaurants, and so… I like a lot of seafood, so, um… my favorite is soft shell crabs...
Q Delicious!
PAT … with steamed vegetables. Maybe I'll have some sort of seafood chowder before that, and a mixed salad, and finish it all with key-lime pie, perhaps.
Q Mmm!

Q Karen, how long have you been living in Hong Kong?
KAREN Just over a year now.
Q And have you gotten used to the way of life there?
KAREN Yes, I think so. It's a very upbeat place, so you have to adapt.
Q Yes, what sort of things do you eat? What's a typical breakfast for you?
KAREN Um… well, during the week I'm very busy. I have to get to the school where I work quite early, so I have just a quick breakfast—but a substantial one. Um… so usually cereal, toast, orange juice, a cup of coffee.
Q Very healthy!
KAREN Uh-huh.
Q Right. And then, er… do you have lunch?
KAREN If I have time, yes. I run out and grab a sandwich, or a baked potato from a local fast-food place, if I can.
Q So, no Chinese delicacies?
KAREN Not at lunch time, no. No time!
Q Yeah, that's not your main meal, then? The main meal is dinner?
KAREN In the evening.
Q Yes, yes. And then, what do you eat?
KAREN Well, um… we get together—several teachers—and we go out to a Chinese restaurant, or um… there is food from all over the world in Hong Kong… Japanese, Indonesian—and we eat there. Um… a favorite Chinese meal is "dim sum."
Q Uh-huh. What's that?
KAREN Well, it's like a dumpling, um… which they steam, and inside are different types of meat or vegetables. They're fantastic.
Q Yes. And, are there any, um… desserts, any sweet things to eat?
KAREN Chinese desserts are very sticky, and a bit too sweet for me, so I usually avoid them.
Q Yeah. Thank you.

Fluency 3 **Speaking and Listening, activity 2**

CLERK Hi there. What can I do for you?

MAN I'd like a pack of Marlboro, please.

CLERK Soft pack or box?

MAN Box, please.

CLERK There you are, one pack of Marlboro. That's two-fifty. Will that be all for you today, sir?

MAN Oh, I need a gallon of milk.

CLERK Right over there in the refrigerator, sir. Help yourself.

MAN Right. And do you have today's paper?

CLERK We sure do. That's fifty cents...and three twenty-nine for the milk, two fifty for the Marlboro...That's six twenty-nine altogether, sir.

MAN Here you are.

CLERK Out of ten? That's thirty, forty, fifty, seven dollars, eight, nine, and ten.

MAN Thanks.

CLERK Thank *you* sir. Have a nice day.

Fluency 3 **Functions, activity 1**

Five hundred and five.

Four hundred and seventy-eight

Three thousand, five hundred and sixty-three.

Forty-five thousand, seven hundred and eighty-one

Fluency 3 **Functions, activity 3**

$10.50

12,314

204

$19.99

138,526

$20.50

Fluency 3 **Speaking and Listening 2, activity 2**

Q OK, Mei and Jorge. I'd like to talk to you about prices of things in your country.

JORGE OK.

MEI OK.

Q First a gallon of milk. How much would a gallon of milk cost in Brazil, Jorge?

JORGE Oh, I guess about $3.

Q And in Malaysia, Mei?

MEI I think about $3.

Q Right. What about a pound of fish?

JORGE I don't know. Perhaps around $1.30.

MEI I think in Malaysia a pound of fish would be about $2.60.

Q OK. How about a meal in a restaurant, Mei?

MEI Well, that depends on the restaurant. I mean there are expensive restaurants and there are cheap restaurants.

Q What about say an average meal for two?

MEI Probably around $20.

JORGE I think in Brazil an average meal for two would cost about $20 to $25.

Q And a bottle of wine?

JORGE Anything from $5 upwards in a supermarket to $10 upwards in a restaurant, depending on how good the wine was.

MEI I guess about $15.

Q Good. Now suppose you want to go to the movies. How much is a ticket for the movies going to cost you?

JORGE Oh, that I know. I go to the movies a lot. In Brazil that would cost you $7.

MEI For us that would be $3.

Q I see. OK. Now you are going to buy a new car. You know, just an ordinary family car. But new, not second-hand. How much?

MEI Probably about $20,000 to $60,000.

JORGE I think in my country it would be anything around $12,000 upwards.

Q Right. Something cheaper now. A newspaper.

MEI That would cost you 50 cents

JORGE In Brazil probably $1.

Q How about ... a new television?

JORGE A new television? Well, I think you could probably buy one for around $350.

Q What about in Malaysia, Mei?

MEI I'm not sure. Maybe for a new television you would have to pay around $200 to $300.

Q OK. Now how about a house? Again I think we're talking about, you know, an average family house, not a huge mansion or anything. Jorge?

JORGE Let me think. I've never bought a house, but I guess you'd have to pay, well, about $200,000.

Q How about you, Mei?

MEI No, I've never bought a house either. I think in Malaysia people pay around $120,000.

Q I see. Quite a difference there! OK, back to cheaper things. How much is a gallon of gas in Brazil, Jorge?

JORGE Gas for the car? Um, I think now it's around $2.26 a gallon.

Q What about a gallon of gas in Malaysia, Mei? How much?

MEI I think around $1.68.

Q Well, that's been very interesting. Thank you both very much.

MEI You're welcome.

JORGE No problem.

Lesson 16 **Listening and Speaking, activity 1**

Q So, Ken, tell me. What is karaoke?

KEN Well, basically, it's singing along to some recorded music. You have a microphone and there's some music playing and you can sing the words—in tune, if you can.

Q Where do you do this?

KEN Well, all over Tokyo there are karaoke bars where you can go with friends, have a drink and sing karaoke. It's very popular.

Q Who does it?

KEN Anyone. Anyone who feels brave enough to sing in public, it could be you or me or anyone.

Q After a couple of beers, maybe! What kind of music do you sing?

KEN Well, it's traditional Japanese music for older people, but for young people it's mostly well-known Western pop songs, you know, Frank Sinatra, Phil Collins, Madonna, that sort of thing.

Q Why do people enjoy it?

KEN I don't know, really. It's a chance to show that you could be a pop singer too, I guess. It's also a way of showing how close you are to your friends. If you can make a fool of yourself in front of these people, then you really are good friends, you know?

Q What about tango, Marybeth?

MARYBETH Tango is a very exotic kind of dance in Latin America, and it's especially popular in Argentina, where it originally came from.

Q And where is it performed?

MARYBETH In concert halls or theaters, or maybe small bars.

Q And who performs the tango?

MARYBETH Well, in the theater they're mostly professional dancers, although in dance halls and bars, everyone tries to dance the tango if the music is right.

Q And what is the music they use?

MARYBETH Well, tango is both the dance and the music. You dance the tango to music specially written for it. They use the violin and the accordion quite a lot for it.

Q And why do you think people enjoy it?

MARYBETH Well, it's a very passionate dance. It's full of life, it's great fun.

Q Can you dance it?

MARYBETH Not real well, but I try!

Lesson 19 **Sounds, activity 1**

1. He's much smarter than I am.
2. She's as intelligent as he is.
3. Her clothes are different from mine.
4. She has the same shoes as I have.
5. Sandals are less common here than in Florida.
6. Kids are more casual than their parents.

Lesson 19 **Sounds, activity 2**

1. He's less casual than she is.
   No, he's *more* casual than she is.
2. It's noisier now than it was.
   No, it's *less* noisy now than it was.
3. Clothes are cheaper here than at home.
   No, clothes are *less* cheap here than at home.
4. He's less optimistic than she is.
   No, he's *more* optimistic than she is.
5. It's easier to get good clothes here.
   No, it's *less* easy to get good clothes here.
6. He's less confident than she is.
   No, he's *more* confident than she is.

Lesson 19 **Listening and Speaking, activity 2**

Q Where are you from originally, Don?
DON Well, I grew up in Valdez, Alaska. My folks still live there, but I moved to New York to study fashion design, and then came here to San Francisco six years ago.
Q Have you traveled much outside of the U.S.?
DON Oh sure! Europe, of course, and Japan, Korea, Thailand—lots of places in Asia. And Mexico, Jamaica, Cuba…
Q Well, how would you describe the way Americans dress?
DON Hmmm. Well, it depends on the season, of course, and the area, but I'd have to say "casual" in general. People dress much more casually in the West than in the East, I think, but jeans are still the most popular clothes, wherever you go—and people wear them for everything.
Q Even to work?
DON Well, I guess it depends on the business, but yes. I guess most people wear suits and ties—formal clothes—for work, and for church, or if they go out for a nice dinner…
Q Are nice clothes expensive?
DON Not really. Not compared to, say, Italy or Japan. But in terms of how much people earn, they're… umm… they're probably about the same, relatively.
Q OK. And what about casual clothes—are they expensive?
DON No, not at all. Did you know a pair of Levis 501s cost three times more in Tokyo than in San Francisco?
Q No kidding! Umm… What do you think of the quality of clothes design in the U.S.?
DON Oh, I think we have some fantastic designers here, not just in terms of fashion, but in terms of practicality and quality.
Q Tell me, would you say Americans are small or large people, compared to other people around the world?
DON Well, uh… there are some really tall people around, and you see a lot more overweight people here than in most other countries. Food is cheap… and good!

Lesson 20 **Listening, activity 1**

Q So, what was your most memorable journey, Sarah?
SARAH Well, in 1990 I drove across country with a friend who was moving home from New Orleans to Laguna Beach on the California coast.
Q Mmm. How long did it take?
SARAH Oh… nine days, I think.
Q What sort of distance is that?
SARAH About 2,500 miles, and that's pretty direct, too.
Q So where did you go?
SARAH Well, we set out from New Orleans and took the Interstate 10

Highway, which runs all the way from Florida to Los Angeles. We got on it just outside the city, and we drove through Louisiana as far as San Antonio in Texas, where we stopped for the night.
Q How far was that?
SARAH Oh, the first day we did 550 miles.
Q What's San Antonio like?
SARAH It's pretty interesting. It's a strange mix of skyscrapers and Indian houses and churches. It's about 200 years old.
Q What's the scenery like in the country? Is it desert or mountainous or what?
SARAH Well, it's not really mountainous at that point, it's um… sort of hills and small trees. It's very remote, though, and you can drive hundreds of miles between gas stations, so you have to make sure you've got plenty of gas.
Q It was cheaper then, wasn't it?
SARAH Yes, it cost about a dollar a gallon, about 40 cents less than now.
Q And, where did you go then?
SARAH Well, after that, we started to hit the desert and we drove 350 miles to Fort Stockton, which is a typical desert motel stop, in the middle of nowhere. Then we drove through the Guadeloupe Mountains National Park to El Paso, on the border between Texas and Mexico. Then between El Paso and Las Cruces you start climbing into the Sierra Madre.
Q And that was when you could only drive at 55 miles an hour?
SARAH Yeah. Of course we went a lot faster. If there were no police patrols around.
Q Where to then?
SARAH We turned off and took a detour to Nogales on the Mexican border which was great. We had lunch there, and then headed north to Tucson, Arizona on Route 19.
Q And where did you stay on the way?
SARAH In motels. They were really cheap. The most expensive was 35 dollars, the cheapest was twenty. And from Tucson we turned west again and crossed into California. From there it's only 300 miles to San Diego on the coast, which was very beautiful—my first sight of the Pacific Ocean. And then we drove on up the Pacific Coast Highway to Laguna Beach, not far from L.A., and arrived at my friend's apartment, with a fabulous sea view and only ten minutes from the beach.
Q It sounds very memorable!
SARAH It was, it really was. But although it was great to arrive, it was much better to travel. We had a blast!

Fluency 4 **Listening and Speaking, activity 2**

A It's my birthday today.
B Congratulations! Did you get any presents?
A Yes, I got a neat pair of socks.
B Socks! What a fantastic present! Anything else?
A Yes, I also got some nice handkerchiefs. They're just what I've always wanted.
B And are you going to do anything to celebrate?
A Yes, I'm going for a walk in the park.
B You sure are celebrating in style! Have a wonderful time.
A Thank you.

Fluency 4 **Listening, activity 1**

Q OK, Judy, can you tell us something about holidays in the United States?

JUDY Sure. Well, I think probably the most important holiday is Thanksgiving. That's always on the last Thursday of November. And it's a time when families get together to say thank you for, well, for all the good things they have enjoyed in the past year. Um, the original Thanksgiving meal was held by the first settlers in the United States. To say thank you to God for their first successful harvest and to say thank you to the Native Americans who helped them survive their first year here.

Q So, basically it's a meal?

JUDY Well, yes, it's the one time in the year when families get together and they cook a big meal, and yes, I think the meal is the most important part of the holiday. We have turkey and pumpkin pie and ...

Q Mmm sounds delicious. How about other holidays? For example when is Labor Day?

JUDY Oh, Labor Day is the first Monday in September. It doesn't commemorate anything in particular, but it's the official end of the summer.

Q And do you do anything special? Are there any special customs on Labor Day?

JUDY No, not really. It's a national holiday so we all have the day off. But there are no special customs or celebrations.

Q How about Valentine's Day?

JUDY Well, that's on February 14th. That's the day when you send a card to the person you love. And it's the day when you can reveal your love to someone who perhaps doesn't know that you love them.

Q And how do you do that?

JUDY Well, traditionally you don't sign the card so the person who gets it has to guess who it's from. And so they find out that there is someone out there who loves them. Sometimes there's a poem in the card. You know, roses are red, violets are blue, this card comes from the one who loves you!

Q Right! Do you give gifts on Valentine's Day?

JUDY Oh, yes, flowers and chocolates usually. And if you're in a relationship, you would probably go out for a romantic dinner.

Q And do Americans know who St. Valentine was?

JUDY I don't think so. I don't think they think about the origins of the day at all. This is just the day when we celebrate being in love. Oh, and it's not really a holiday—you don't get the day off—it's just another working day.

Q OK. Another big holiday is Independence Day, July 4th. Can you tell us something about that?

JUDY Yes, of course, Independence Day is a big holiday. It's when we celebrate our Independence from Britain, you know after the War of Independence in 1776, when the United States first became an independent country. It's in the summer on July 4th so we have picnics and ball games, fireworks, parades. It's really quite something.

Q Finally, what about Mother's Day. Is that big in the States?

JUDY Oh, yes, that's big over here. Particularly for the flower sellers.

Q So you give flowers to your mom?

JUDY Oh, yes, we give flowers and cards and sometimes a present. To say thank you to our mom for having raised us and looked after us all those years.

Q And when is Mother's Day?

JUDY Well, I think it's the second Sunday in May.

Q Well, thanks very much.

JUDY You're welcome.

Progress Test 1 Lessons 1–10

SECTION 1: VOCABULARY (30 points)

1. a. Underline the word which doesn't belong and leave a group of three related words. (10 points)

b. Add one other word to the groups of words. (10 points)

Example: her my our <u>they</u> *their*

1. after always often sometimes _____

2. afternoon morning night yesterday

   _____

3. bath refrigerator shower sink _____

4. aunt cousin husband tourist _____

5. cathedral countryside factory park

   _____

6. crowded friendly generous polite

   _____

7. children man students women _____

8. did lived see wrote _____

9. American France Germany Japan

   _____

10. dirty expensive modern safety _____

2. Complete these sentences with ten different verbs. (10 points)

Example: I _*buy*_ food at the supermarket.

1. I never _____ shopping.

2. She doesn't _____ a musical instrument.

3. I _____ to music at home.

4. Pleased to _____ you.

5. Where do you _____ from?

6. I _____ about ten cigarettes a day.

7. Where do we _____ for the bus?

8. I can't _____ the weather in Hawaii.

9. Where do you _____ dinner?

10. They don't _____ glasses.

Progress Test 1 Lessons 1–10

SECTION 2: GRAMMAR (30 points)

3. a. Choose ten of these words to complete the first ten spaces in the passage. (10 points)

Example: a) had b) has c) have

1. a) go b) was c) went
2. a) cousin b) cousins c) cousin's
3. a) a b) an c) the
4. a) because b) but c) so
5. a) get b) got c) has
6. a) has b) is c) isn't
7. a) a b) one c) two
8. a) from b) in c) to
9. a) because b) but c) so
10. a) aren't b) weren't c) didn't

b. Complete the last ten spaces with ten of your own words. (10 points)

When did I last ___have___ a vacation? Well, six months ago I (1) _____ to the Southwest because my (2) _____ is out there. He's (3) _____ engineer. He lives and works in Denver (4) _____ I decided to visit him there. Denver's an interesting city and it (5)_____ lots of theaters and art galleries. There aren't many tourists and it (6) _____ very expensive. After (7) _____ days in Denver, we took a plane (8) _____ Las Vegas. We had one way tickets (9) _____ we wanted to drive back to Denver.

Our first stop was the Grand Canyon. There is a hotel in Grand Canyon village but we (10) _____ stay at the hotel. The weather (11) _____ awful but we decided to walk to the bottom of the canyon. There is a hostel at the bottom of the canyon (12) _____ we stayed there. There (13) _____ beds for about thirty people in the hostel and there (14) _____ a kitchen and a dining room. You pay about $50 per person and (15) _____ have dinner and breakfast there. I come from Philadelphia and I (16) _____

some people from my hometown in the hostel. The hostel was full and (17) _____ were lots of Japanese people there. I (18) _____ Japanese people because they're so friendly and polite. The next day we had breakfast (19) _____ seven o'clock and checked out at seven-thirty. Then we walked back to (20) _____ village and had lunch in the hotel.

4. Write your own questions for these answers. (10 points)

Example: Yes, I am. This is my husband.
Are you married?

1. I'm twenty-three.

   _____

2. I'm an engineer.

   _____

3. Fine, thanks.

   _____

4. At a quarter after seven in the morning.

   _____

5. Yes, one brother and two sisters.

   _____

6. We usually go abroad.

   _____

7. I watched TV, and then I went to bed.

   _____

8. I'm writing a letter.

   _____

9. No, there isn't.

   _____

10. I'd like a beer, please.

    _____

77

SECTION 3: READING (20 points)

5. Read the passage *At Home in the Land of the Rising Sun*. Which of these things is the article about? Check the box. (2 points)

a. Traditional Japanese homes. ☐

b. The differences between modern and traditional Japanese homes. ☐

c. Traditional features of modern Japanese homes. ☐

6. Are these sentences true (T) or false (F) or doesn't the passage say (DS)? (10 points)

Example: Japanese bathrooms are quite small. `DS`

1. People eat and sleep in separate rooms. ☐

2. A typical Japanese home has cushions and curtains. ☐

3. There are often dried grass mats in Japanese homes. ☐

4. All Japanese apartments have gardens. ☐

5. Japanese gardens are always very small. ☐

7. Find four things the passage says about hospitality in Japan. Make notes. (8 points)

_____

_____

_____

_____

_____

_____

_____

AT HOME IN THE LAND OF THE RISING SUN

Many people in Japan now live in apartments and their homes have all the latest household equipment. But there are still many old and traditional features in modern Japanese homes.

The *genkan,* or hall, is always an important feature in Japanese homes. It is usually where the family and guests change their shoes. It is a place of welcome and often has flowers or a picture. When guests leave, everyone goes to the *genkan* to say goodbye.

The main room of a Japanese home is used as the sitting room, dining room, and bedroom, and there isn't much furniture, just cushions around a low table. Other features are *oshiire*, or cupboards, where you put bedding and clothes during the day, *fusuma* or sliding doors to make the living areas into a number of small rooms, and many homes still have a *tokonoma*, a small area with flowers, a painting, and a *tatami* mat. Guests usually sit in front of the *tokonoma*. The kitchen is often very small, and you never eat or entertain people there.

Modern building materials are of course very common, but there is still some wood and paper in modern homes. There are often bamboo curtains *(sudare)* and heavy wooden shutters *(amado)* on the windows. The most common feature is the *tatami* mat, made of dried grass, about 5' by 3'. The Japanese still measure a room by the number of *tatami* mats it can contain.

A garden is very important, if the home has enough space. It is not a place where children play but somewhere beautiful to look at. If there isn't a garden, there are pots of plants or small bonsai trees on shelves.

SECTION 4: WRITING (20 points)

8. Introduce yourself to your teacher. For example, include some information about your home and family, describe your daily routine, and / or say what you like doing. Write 10–15 sentences. (20 points)

_____

_____

_____

_____

_____

_____

_____

_____

_____

_____

_____

_____

_____

_____

_____

_____

_____

_____

_____

_____

_____

Photocopiable

Progress Test 2 Lessons 11–20

SECTION 1: VOCABULARY (30 points)

1. a. Find fifteen words in the word square. The words are in two directions: ↓ and →. Write the words in five groups. (15 points)

A. jobs _____

_____

B. subjects _____

_____

C. clothes _____

_____

D. town features _____

_____

E. things to eat _____

_____

J	E	C	O	N	O	M	I	C	S
O	H	S	S	O	N	I	O	N	S
U	I	T	W	S	U	I	T	H	P
R	S	A	E	N	B	N	M	O	O
N	T	D	A	U	R	Y	U	S	T
A	O	I	T	R	E	L	S	P	A
L	R	U	E	S	A	O	E	I	T
I	Y	M	R	E	D	N	U	T	O
S	A	C	T	O	R	S	M	A	E
T	S	C	I	E	N	C	E	L	S

b. Add one other word to each group of words in 1a. (5 points)

2. Complete these sentences with ten different nouns. (10 points)

Example:
There's an _intermission_ of 15 minutes during the concert.

1. I'd like to earn a lot of _____ .

2. How many _____ of cookies do we need?

3. The seats are in the third _____ on the left.

4. He's got long hair, a _____, and a moustache.

5. He's wearing _____ because he's going running.

6. Does _____ cost $2 a gallon?

7. Is there any _____ in your medical kit?

8. I have a _____ so I don't need scissors.

9. There's an _____ of her work at the gallery.

10. There was a driver and three _____ in the car.

Progress Test 2   Lessons 11–20

SECTION 2: GRAMMAR (30 points)

3. a. Choose ten of these words to complete the first ten spaces in the conversation. (10 points)

Example: a) go b) going c) to go
1. a) for b) in c) on
2. a) can't b) don't c) won't
3. a) at b) in c) on
4. a) last b) next c) this
5. a) at b) in c) on
6. a) see b) seeing c) to see
7. a) best b) better c) good
8. a) does b) is c) will
9. a) many b) much c) often
10. a) I'll call b) I'm going to call c) I'm calling

b. Complete the last ten spaces with ten of your own words. (10 points)

SANDRA: How about _going_ to the theater
(1) _____ the weekend?

DENISE: I'm sorry, I (2) _____ . I'm going to my
sister's place (3) _____ Reno tomorrow for the
weekend. What about some evening (4) _____
week?

SANDRA: OK. How about Wednesday?

DENISE: That's fine. What's (5) _____ ?

SANDRA: *A Comedy of Errors* is at the Playhouse. I saw
it a year ago but I'd like (6) _____ it again. I
think it's Shakespeare's (7) _____ play.

DENISE: What time (8) _____ it start?

SANDRA: Seven-thirty.

DENISE: How (9) _____ are the tickets?

SANDRA: I don't know.

DENISE: (10) _____ the theater and find out. I'm
sure they (11) _____ be very expensive. I'll
reserve two seats, (12) _____ you like. Where is
the Playhouse, by the way?

SANDRA: It's in Jarrett Street. You know the bus station?
Well, go down First, (13) _____ left at the
intersection, and then take the second
(14) _____ the right. It's next (15) _____ the

parking lot.

DENISE: How (16) _____ is it from the bus station?

SANDRA: About five hundred yards. It (17) _____
about ten minutes on foot. But, listen, I'm going to
drive. I don't (18) _____ using public
transportation late (19) _____ night. I'll give
you a ride. I'll pick you (20) _____ at about
seven o'clock.

DENISE: Great! Thanks a lot.

4. Rewrite these sentences. Begin with the words in parentheses. (10 points)

Example: She's more patient than he is. (He is)
He is less patient than she is.

1. The post office is across from the library.
(The library)

   _____

2. I bought a guidebook because I'm going to Mexico
City. (I'm going)

   _____

3. Could you tell me the way to the courthouse?
(How do)

   _____

4. How about going to the opera next week? (Let's)

   _____

5. She isn't as confident as he is. (He)

   _____

6. The T-shirts are cheaper than the shirts.
(The shirts)

   _____

7. The drugstore is behind the grocery store.
(The grocery store)

   _____

8. Fruit is better for you than chocolate.
(Chocolate isn't)

   _____

9. He's completely bald. (He doesn't)

   _____

10. She likes going to university. (She enjoys)

   _____

Photocopiable

Progress Test 2 Lessons 11–20

SECTION 3: READING (20 points)

5. Read the passage *Highway to the Andes*. Was James Ferguson's journey terrible? (2 points)

_____

6. Are these sentences true (T) or false (F) or doesn't the passage say (DS)? (8 points)

Example: James began his journey in Valencia. [F]

1. Most people fly from Caracas to Mérida. [ ]

2. James ate roast beef on his journey. [ ]

3. Caracas is two hundred and ninety miles from Barinas. [ ]

4. Barinas is higher than 9,800 feet. [ ]

5. People say that the first part of the journey is the best. [ ]

6. James stopped for a drink in the *páramo*. [ ]

7. Mérida is 15,700 feet above sea level. [ ]

8. He tried a garlic-flavored ice cream. [ ]

7. What did James see out of his car window? Use these five headings and make notes. (10 points)

a. near Caracas

_____

_____

b. near Valencia

_____

_____

c. near Acarigua

_____

_____

d. near Apartaderos

_____

_____

e. near Mérida

_____

_____

Highway to the Andes

"You're going to DRIVE to Mérida? But it's so far—it will be terrible." This is what my friends said when I told them I wanted to go to Mérida by car.

The Venezuelans love taking planes. Domestic flights are reliable and cheap and there are lots of them. So people thought it a little strange that I wanted to hire a car and drive, what is only 450 miles, to the Andean city of Mérida.

But the journey wasn't terrible at all. The roads were in good condition, there was a freeway for part of the way, and regular gas stations (where gas cost less than water). There was even a roadside self-service restaurant between Caracas and Valencia.

I drove out of Caracas, and its mixture of modern skyscrapers and old, poor housing, on a mountainous highway. At first, the scenery was Caribbean: bananas, small villages, coconut trees. When you reach Valencia, orange trees mix with sugar-cane. A little further on, past Acarigua, the country changes into the *llanos* or plains. This is real cowboy country, with huge isolated farms and occasional roadside ovens where you can buy roast beef by the pound.

Everyone agrees that the last four hours to Mérida are the best, so it's a good idea to spend the night in Barinas and drive the remaining 160 miles in the morning. An hour or so out of Barinas and the Andes seem to appear suddenly around the corner. From then on, it's an exciting climb up to 9,800 feet and the Venezuelan *páramo*.

The *páramo* is the cold, windy mountain range. Although there are no trees in these mountains, there are lots of plants and flowers. At 11,800 feet you notice that the air is getting thinner. After a strong cup of Venezuelan coffee at the village of Apartaderos, my heart seemed to beat much faster than usual.

My car didn't like the thin air and slowed down. I didn't mind—this gave me time to look at the mountains. Locally, "crossing the *páramo*" means dying, and the car seemed to know this.

The scenery on the way down into Mérida is spectacular. Some of it is Andean with its low, stone villages and potato fields, and some is Alpine with its rivers full of fish, and inviting hotels. Mérida itself is a pleasant town. It has three claims to fame: the University of the Andes, the world's highest cable-car—to the snowy 15,700-foot Pico Bolívar—and an ice cream shop with the world's largest number of flavors (400), including garlic and spaghetti bolognese. But this wasn't why I had come.

Adapted from *Highway to the Andes* by James Ferguson.

Progress Test 2 Lessons 11–20

SECTION 4: WRITING (20 points)

8. Describe someone you know well. For example, talk about the person's clothes, appearance, and character. Write 10–15 sentences.

_____

_____

_____

_____

_____

_____

_____

_____

_____

_____

_____

_____

_____

_____

_____

_____

_____

_____

_____

Photocopiable

Answers Progress Test 1 Lessons 1–10

SECTION 1: VOCABULARY [30 points]

1. a. (10 points: 1 point for each correct answer.)

1. after	6. crowded
2. yesterday	7. man
3. refrigerator	8. see
4. tourist	9. American
5. countryside	10. safety

b. (10 points: 1 point for each appropriate answer.)
1. an adverb of frequency, e.g. *never, usually*
2. evening (expression of time used with *in the*)
3. toilet (equipment found in a bathroom)
4. a family member, e.g. *brother, grandfather*
5. a feature or facility of towns, e.g. *restaurant, university*
6. an adjective for describing people, e.g. *awful, unfriendly*
7. a plural noun, e.g. *chairs, men*
8. a past tense form, e.g. *had, walked*
9. the name of a country, e.g. *United States, Saudi Arabia*
10. an adjective for describing aspects of towns, e.g. *boring, safe*

2. (10 points: 1 point for each appropriate answer.)

1. go	6. smoke
2. play	7. wait
3. listen	8. stand
4. meet	9. have
5. come	10. wear

SECTION 2: GRAMMAR [30 points]

3. a. (10 points: 1 point for each correct answer.)

1. c) went	6. c) isn't
2. a) cousin	7. c) two
3. b) an	8. c) to
4. c) so	9. a) because
5. c) has	10. c) didn't

b. (10 points: 1 point for each appropriate answer.)
Possible answers

11. was	16. met
12. and/so	17. there
13. are	18. like/love
14. is	19. at
15. you	20. the

4. (10 points: 1 point for each correct question.)
Possible answers
1. How old are you?
2. What do you do?
3. How are you?
4. What time do you get up/ have breakfast/go to work?
5. Do you have any brothers and sisters?
6. Where do you go on vacation?
7. What did you do yesterday evening/last night?
8. What are you doing/writing?
9. Is there a dining room in your house?
10. What would you like (to drink)?

SECTION 3: READING [20 points]

5. (2 points)
c

6. (10 points: 2 points for each correct answer.)

1. F	4. F
2. T	5. DS
3. T	

7. (8 points: 2 points for each of the four things.)
1. Guests change their shoes in the *genkan*.
2. When guests leave, everyone goes to the *genkan* to say goodbye.
3. Guests usually sit in front of the *tokonoma*.
4. You never eat or entertain people in the kitchen.

SECTION 4: WRITING [20 points]

8. (20 points)
Tell students what you will take into consideration when grading their written work. Criteria should include:
- efficient communication of meaning (7 points)
- grammatical accuracy (7 points)
- coherence in the ordering or the information or ideas (3 points)
- layout, capitalization, and punctuation (3 points)

It is probably better not to use a rigid grading system with the written part of the test. If, for example, you always deduct a point for a grammatical mistake, you may find that you are over-penalizing students who write a lot or who take risks. Deduct points if students haven't written the minimum number of sentences stated in the test.

Answers Progress Test 2 Lessons 11–20

SECTION 1: VOCABULARY [30 points]

1. a. (15 points: 1 point for each correct answer.)
- A. jobs: actor, journalist, nurse
- B. subjects: economics, history, science
- C. clothes: suit, sweater, nylons
- D. town features: hospital, museum, stadium
- E. things to eat: bread, onions, potatoes

b. (5 points: 1 point for each appropriate answer.)

2. (10 points: 1 point for each appropriate answer.)
1. money
2. packages
3. row
4. beard
5. sneakers
6. gas
7. aspirin
8. pocketknife
9. exhibition
10. passengers

SECTION 2: GRAMMAR [30 points]

3. a. (10 points: 1 point for each correct answer.)
1. c) on
2. a) can't
3. b) in
4. b) next
5. c) on
6. c) to see
7. a) best
8. a) does
9. b) much
10. a) I'll call

b. (10 points: 1 point for each appropriate answer.)
Possible answers
11. won't
12. if
13. turn
14. on
15. to
16. far
17. takes
18. like
19. at
20. up

4. (10 points: 1 point for each correct sentence.)
1. The library is across from the post office.
2. I'm going to Mexico City, so I bought a guidebook.
3. How do I get to the courthouse?
4. Let's go to the opera next week.
5. He's more confident than she is.
6. The shirts are more expensive than the T-shirts. / The shirts aren't as cheap as the T-shirts.
7. The grocery store is in front of the drugstore.
8. Chocolate isn't as good for you as fruit.
9. He doesn't have any hair.
10. She enjoys going to university.

SECTION 3: READING [20 points]

5. (2 points)
no

6. (8 points: 1 point for each correct answer.)
1. T
2. DS
3. T
4. F
5. F
6. T
7. F
8. DS

7. (10 points: 2 points for the notes under each heading.)
a. near Caracas: bananas, villages, coconut trees
b. near Valencia: orange trees, sugar cane
c. near Acarigua: farms, cowboys, roadside ovens
d. near Apartaderos: plants, flowers
e. near Mérida: villages, potato fields, rivers, hotels

SECTION 4: WRITING [20 points]

8. (20 points)
Tell students what you will take into consideration when grading their written work. Criteria should include:
- efficient communication of meaning (7 points)
- grammatical accuracy (7 points)
- coherence in the ordering or the information or ideas (3 points)
- layout, capitalization, and punctuation (3 points)

It is probably better not to use a rigid grading system with the written part of the test. If, for example, you always deduct a point for a grammatical mistake, you may find that you are over-penalizing students who write a lot or who take risks. Deduct points if students haven't written the minimum number of sentences stated in the test.

Practice Book Answer Key

Lesson 1

READING
2. Ask: "What should I call you?"

VOCABULARY
1. Across: 1. help 4. where
5. family 7. are 8. meet
10. first 11. do 13. understand
Down: 1. hello 2. please
3. repeat 5. from 6. married
9. is 12. old
2. 1. e 2. c 3. a 4. b 5. d
3. Across: want sing go visit
live talk
Down: arrive think stay
take offer drink ask sit
accept

GRAMMAR
1. 1. visit 2. take 3. talk
4. ask 5. drink 6. go
3. 1. I never offer to do the dishes.
2. I always arrive about ten
minutes late.
3. I usually take wine or
chocolates.
4. I sometimes drink coffee
after the meal.
5. I don't often go to dinner
parties on my own.
6. I don't usually wear nice
clothes.
4. *Possible Answers*
Are you American?
Where do you live?
What do you do?
Are you married?
What's your name?

Lesson 2

VOCABULARY
1. 1. seven P.M. / seven o'clock in
the evening
2. one fifteen A.M. / a quarter
after one in the morning
3. two forty-five P.M. / a quarter
to three in the afternoon
4. nine thirty A.M. / half past
nine in the morning
5. eleven forty-five P.M. /
a quarter to twelve at night
6. eight ten A.M. / ten after eight
in the morning
2. *Possible Answers*
1. I wake up 2. I get up
3. I have breakfast 4. I get
ready for school/work
5. I leave home
6. I have lunch 7. I come
home 8. I have dinner
9. I watch TV 10. I go to sleep

GRAMMAR
1. 1. goes 2. works 3. finish
4. sits 5. doesn't 6. watch
7. offer 8. don't
3. 1. up 2. home 3. lunch
4. and 5. doesn't 6. day
4. 1. gets 2. has 3. does
4. watches 5. gets 6. goes

READING AND WRITING
1. Photo 3.
2. At 8:30 A.M. she leaves home.
At 12:30 P.M. she stops for
lunch.
At 6:00 P.M. she eats dinner.
At 10:30 P.M. she goes to bed.

Lesson 3

GRAMMAR
1. 1. – 2. a 3. the 4. the 5. a
6. – 7. the 8. an 9. –
10. the 11. an 12. a 13. –
14. an 15. the 16. a 17. the
18. a 19. the 20. the
4. 1. buses 2. curtains 3. classes
4. families 5. parties 6. plays
7. sandwiches 8. shoes
9. windows 10. women

READING AND VOCABULARY
1. a. 3 b. 6 c. 5 d. 1 e. 4
f. 7 g. 2
2. 1. region or country where a
person was born 2. a house
where old people live and are
taken care of 3. the place
where a person lives 4. a
game on the team's own
ground 5. find a place to keep
things 6. confident and able
7. a place where someone feels
very happy and relaxed.

Lesson 4

READING AND WRITING
2. 1. radio 2. long lines
3. winter 4. newspapers
5. gardening

VOCABULARY
1. awful cheap cold crowded dirty
friendly great polite slow warm
2. 1. crowded 2. driving
3. food 4. friendly 5. litter
6. cheap

GRAMMAR
2. *Possible Answers*
1. visiting 2. going to
3. having 4. listening to
5. having 6. going 7. drinking
8. playing

Lesson 5

GRAMMAR
1. 1. ask 2. carry 3. go
4. watch 5. come 6. leave
7. shine 8. write 9. get
10. sit 11. stop 12. travel
2. 1. c 2. f 3. a 4. e 5. d 6. b
3. 1. wears / is wearing 2. works
/ is working 3. drink / am
drinking 4. am having / have
5. watches / is watching
6. read / am reading

VOCABULARY
1. 1. N 2. V 3. V 4. V 5. N
6. N

READING AND WRITING
1. A. 1 B. 5 C. 12 D. 10
2. E. A woman is talking on the
phone.
F. A man is writing a letter.
G. A man and a woman are
dancing.
H. A girl is riding a bicycle.

Lesson 6

GRAMMAR
1. 1. started 2. named 3. lived
4. watched 5. asked
6. opened
2. 1. didn't play 2. didn't like
3. didn't look 4. didn't dance
5. didn't stay 6. didn't want
3. Past simple: left said gave
told built did got thought
came knew
Infinitive: buy have need
sleep hear run sit take
be make
4. Past simple: bought had
needed slept heard ran sat
took was/were made
Infinitive: leave say give tell
build do get think come
know
5. 1. PA 2. PR 3. PA 4. PR
5. PA 6. PR

VOCABULARY
1. 1. built; bridge 2. wrote;
check 3. big lake 4. million;
city 5. expensive house
6. desert; dry

READING
1. a female deer
2. 1. the noise of the motorbike.
2. the motorbike hit her. 3. fell
to the ground. 4. disappeared
into the trees. 5. she started to
walk home.
3. the animal: she was trembling
with fear; her heart was beating,
frightened
the writer: happy, excited; my
head was full of the unexpected
meeting with the animal

Lesson 7

VOCABULARY
1. 1. I took a taxi to the airport.
2. I cashed my traveler's check
at the bank.
3. She carried cash in her
purse.
4. He decided to take a trip to
Europe.
5. An American tourist wanted
the blanket.
6. She signed her name on the
top line.
2. See the underlined words above.
3. *Possible Answers*
traveler's check, foreign country,
bank account, credit card, major
currencies, trip abroad

READING AND GRAMMAR
1. 1. f 2. c 3. h 4. g 5. b
6. d 7. a 8. e.
3. 1. the *Titanic*
2. the moon
3. Charles Lindbergh
4. Marco Polo
5. the South Pole
6. Sir Edmund Hillary and
Sherpa Tenzing reached the top
of Everest
7. 1955
8. Jules Verne
4. 2. Who went to the moon in
1969?
3. What did Charles Lindbergh
do in 1927?
4. Where did Marco Polo go in
the 12th century?
5. Who went to the South Pole
in 1912?
6. When did Hillary and
Tenzing reach the top of
Everest?
7. What opened to the public
in 1955?
8. What did Jules Verne write?

Lesson 8

VOCABULARY
1. *Possible Answers*
plane: airport, flight attendant,
airline ticket
train: station, conductor, ticket,
track
car: gas, wheels, driver,
pollution
bicycle: helmet, exercise, ride,
healthy

GRAMMAR
1. 1. got 2. took 3. got
4. went 5. had/ate 6. wrote
7. went 8. ate 9. took
10. saw 11. was 12. came
13. made/cooked
14. had/found 15. had
16. left/went 17. was

2. *Possible Answers*
1. He didn't stay in bed late.
2. He didn't take a bath.
3. He didn't drive to the post office.
4. He didn't have lunch with his brother and his family.
5. He didn't take his nephews to a park.
6. He didn't go out for dinner in the evening.
4. 1. b, e   2. d, a   3. c, f

READING AND WRITING
1. 3, 5, 4, 1, 2

Lesson 9

READING
2. 1 N   2 N   3 N   4 N   5 N
Kathy doesn't actually give the answers to any of the questions.
3. The text gives clues to some of the answers:
1. don't know   2. probably five: Kathy, her husband and three children   3. probably three   4. don't know
5. Greek-Australian, but probably more Greek than Australian

VOCABULARY
♀ aunt   girlfriend   daughter   mother   girl   grandmother   wife   niece   sister   woman

○ uncle   boyfriend   son   father   boy   grandfather   husband   nephew   brother   man

GRAMMAR
2. 1. He is my father.
2. We are your brothers.
3. I am her cousin.
4. They are our girlfriends.
5. She is his wife.
6. You are their nephews.
3. 1. S   2. P   3. P   4. S   5. P
6. P   7. S   8. S
4. 1. sister's   2. brother's
3. cousins'   4. friends'   5. sisters'
6. nephew's
5. *Possible Answers*
2. Do you have any sisters?
3. Do you live alone or with your parents?
4. What size family do you come from?
5. Do you have any cousins?
6. Are your grandparents still alive?
7. Are you the oldest of the brothers and sisters in your family?
8. How often do the members of your family get together?

Lesson 10

READING
1. 1. Kalo Chorio   2. Aghios Nikolaos   3. Kalo Chorio
4. Kalo Chorio
2. 1. It has three.
2. Yes, they do.
3. It has one post office.
4. Kalo Chorio doesn't have a market.

GRAMMAR
1. 1. How many supermarkets does Aghios Nikolaos have?
2. Does Aghios Nikolaos have a doctor?
3. Does Kalo Chorio have any beaches?
4. Does Aghios Nikolaos have a post office?
2. 1. has   2. have   3. has
4. have   5. have   6. has
3. 2. We've   3. Madrid's
5. They've

WRITING
1. 1. The architecture is interesting but the streets are dirty.
2. The subways are safe and clean.
3. It's got excellent but expensive restaurants.
4. It's crowded and dangerous.
5. It's got a couple of parks but it hasn't got any swimming pools.
6. The stores are cheap but crowded.
2. Here we are in Kalo Chorio. We're having a wonderful time (1) and the weather's great. Martin's nice and brown, (6) but I'm just red. We've got a nice apartment, (5) and it's only a five–minute walk from the stores and tavernas. There isn't much to do here, (2) but it's very relaxing. There's only one disco, (4) but there are quite a lot of bars. We're sitting in Pinnochio's (3) and having a drink and a barbecue. Hope all's well at home. See you soon.
Love, Diane x x

Lesson 11

GRAMMAR
1. 1. ...so I'm going to start saving some money
2. ...so I'm going to teach myself a foreign language.
3. ...so I'm going to do some serious training.
4. ...so I'm not going to eat junk food.
5. ...so I'm going to phone the airport and see if they give lessons.
6. ... so I'm going to look at the ads in tomorrow's paper.
2. 1. I'm going to start saving some money because I'd like to buy a horse.
2. I'm going to teach myself a foreign language because I'd like to work abroad.
3. I'm going to do some serious training because I'd like to run a marathon.
4. I'm not going to eat junk food because I'd like to lose some weight.
5. I'm going to phone the airport and see if they give lessons because I'd like to try parachuting.
6. I'm going to look at the ads

in tomorrow's paper because I'd like to change my job.
4. *Possible Answers*
1. Are you going to learn to drive?
2. Are you going to get up late this weekend?
3. What are you going to do?
4. Are you going to catch a bus?
5. Are you going to watch it?
6. When are you going to clean it up?
5. 1. to go   2. to have
3. studying   4. to change
5. to live   6. doing

WRITING
1. She's going to Japan because she'd like to improve her Japanese by living with a Japanese family.

VOCABULARY AND READING
3. 1. d   2. a   3. b   4. c

Lesson 12

READING
1. 2. Is the United States an English-Speaking Country?
3. 1. F   2. F   3. T   4. T   5. T
4. Santa Claus   Dutch
prairie   French
dumb   German
tycoon   Japanese
raccoon   Native American
buffalo   Spanish

VOCABULARY
1. *Possible Answers*
accountant: math
doctor: biology, chemistry, physics, science
engineer: chemistry, math, algebra, physics
journalist: economics, geography, history, languages
politician: economics, geography, history, languages
secretary: languages

GRAMMAR
1. 1. I'll   3. They'll   4. I'll
2. 1. I think Susan will become rich and famous.
2. I think Pete will get married in September.
3. I think Katie will decide to leave home.
4. I think Bill will learn another foreign language.
5. I think Eddie will make some new friends.
6. I think Joanna will start her own business.

Lesson 13

GRAMMAR
1. 1. I'll   2. She's going to   3. I'll
4. are you going to; We're going to   5. We'll   6. He'll
2. 1. this evening   2. tomorrow morning   3. the day after tomorrow   4. in three days
5. next month   6. in a year
4. 1. 'll   2. won't   3. won't   4. 'll
5. won't   6. 'll
5. 1. I won't eat so much fast food.

2. I'll be early for classes.
3. I'll be less pessimistic.
4. I won't drive to work.
5. I'll go to bed earlier.
6. I won't watch so much television.
6. 1. won't   2. 'll   3. won't   4. 'll
5. 'll   6. won't
8. 1. going to   2. will   3. going to   4. will
9. 1. I'm going to visit my grandparents on the weekend.
2. I'll make you a drink.
3. My dad's going to phone at six o'clock.
4. She'll be late.

Lesson 14

READING
3. 1. The White House
2. The Lincon Memorial
3. The Washington Monument
4. The Vietnam Veterans Memorial
5. The Jefferson Memorial
4. a. 132–the number of rooms in the White House
b. 19–the height (in feet) of the statues of Lincoln and Jefferson
c. 555–the height (in feet) of the Washington Monument
d. 58,000–the number of Americans killed in the Vietnam War
e. 50–the number of states in the United States

VOCABULARY
1. art gallery–National Gallery of Art
law courts–Supreme Court
library–Library of Congress
museum–Smithsonian, National Museum of American History, National Air and Space Museum, National Museum of Natural History
park–West Potomac Park, Constitution Gardens
river–Potomac
train station–Union Station

GRAMMAR
1. *Possible Answers*
The Smithsonian Institute is on Jefferson Drive, across from the National Museum of Natural History.
The Supreme Court is between 1st and 2nd Street, behind the Capitol.
The Ellipse is between E Street and Constitution Avenue, in front of the White House.
The National Air and Space Museum is on Jefferson Drive, across from the National Gallery of Art.
2. 1. straight   2. left   3. right
4. left   5. right   6. on   7. right
3. *Possible Answers*
1. Turn right on Jefferson Avenue and go to the end. Turn left and go up to Constitution Avenue, then turn right. Turn left onto Louisiana Avenue, and go straight to the

Photocopiable

end. Union Station is right in front of you.

2. Turn left on Jefferson Avenue and go straight until you get to 14th Street. Cross the street, and walk straight through the park, past the Washington Memorial. Cross over 17th Street, and continue west to the Reflecting Pool. The Lincoln Memorial is right in front of you, on 23rd Street.

3. Walk east through the park until you get to 14th Street. Turn left and take the first right onto Madison Drive. Go down to the end of Madison Drive, and turn left. Turn right onto Constitution Avenue and keep walking until you get to 1st Street. Turn right, and the Supreme Court Building is on the right.

Lesson 15

VOCABULARY

1. 1. lettuce 2. fish 3. apple 4. vegetable 5. juice 6. bread
2. 1. apple, onion, orange, egg
   2. beer, water, juice, milk, wine
   3. coffee, butter, tea
   4. coffee, tea
   5. beef, chicken, lamb, apple, carrot, potato, banana, orange, peach, cheese, egg, bread
   6. beef, chicken, lamb, apple, carrot, potato, banana, orange, peach, cheese, egg, bread
3. 1. an egg, some eggs, some egg
   2. some bananas, some banana, a banana
   3. some chickens, a chicken, some chicken
   4. an onion, some onion, some onions

GRAMMAR

1. 1. I'd like 2. He's having 3. I'm eating 4. I like 5. Would you 6. We drink
2. 1. How many should I get?
   2.. How much do we need?
   3. How many would you like?
   4. How much have you got?
   5. How much should we get?
3. 1. some. We don't need any apples.
   2. any. I have some lettuce.
   3 any. He needs some eggs.
   4. some. She doesn't have any fish.
   5. some. I don't need any milk.
4. two, some, any, How many, any, some, any, How much, carton, some, some, package, bottle

Lesson 16

GRAMMAR

1. at: half past five, night, three o'clock, lunchtime
   in: August, 1994, the morning, winter
   on: Friday evening, November 2nd, the weekend, Wednesday

3. 1. Let's go shopping on Saturday morning.
   2. How about going to a movie in the afternoon?
   3. Why don't we have dinner in the evening?
   4. Would you like to try the new Brazilian restaurant?
6. 1. I 2. I'd 3. I
   4. I 5. I'd 6. I

READING AND VOCABULARY

1. 1. c 2. d 3. b 4. e 5. a
2. 1. movie 2. musical
   3. exhibition 4. ballet
3. 1. F 2. T 3. F 4. F
   5. T 6. F 7. T 8. F

Lesson 17

VOCABULARY

1. appearance: attractive, good-looking, pretty, slim, tall, ugly
   character: calm, confident, intelligent, nervous, quiet, thoughtful
2. Across: 3. lazy 4. beard
   5. medium 7. fat 8. slim
   9. shy 10. curly
   Down: 1. old 2. patient
   6. ugly 7. fair 8. short
3. 1. She has long hair. It's fair and straight. She's tall and thin.
   2. He has a moustache and a beard. He's bald. He's short and fat.
   3. She's medium-height and middle-aged. She has dark, curly hair and glasses.
4. He has dark hair and a beard. He's tall, slim, and good-looking.
5. *Example answer*
   She's short and slim. She has white hair and glasses.

GRAMMAR

1. 1. How long's her hair?
   2. How old is she?
   3. Who's she like?
   4. What does she look like?
   5. Who does he look like?
   6. What's he like?
   7. How tall is he?
   8. What color's his hair?
3. 2 How old is he/she?
   3. How long's his/her hair?
   4. What does he/she look like?
   5. Who does she look like?
   6. What color's his hair?

Lesson 18

READING

1. The writer is an American. She says "we".
2. friendly emotional loud polite informal

VOCABULARY

2. calm–nervous;
   careful–careless;
   honest–dishonest;
   kind–unkind;
   tidy–untidy;
   patient–impatient;
   polite–impolite;

quiet–noisy;
respectful–disrespectful;
thoughtful–thoughtless
3. 1. forty; 2. thirty, thirty-five, forty-nine; 3. seventeen; 4. forty, twenty; 5. twenty-five, fifty; 6. fifty

GRAMMAR

1.

adjective	comparative	superlative
1. bad	worse	worst
2. tall	taller	tallest
3. close	closer	closest
4. good	better	best
5. friendly	friendlier	friendliest
6. kind	kinder	kindest
7. nervous	more nervous	most nervous
8. nice	nicer	nicest
9. sensitive	more sensitive	most sensitive
10. smart	smarter	smartest

2. 1. bad 2. taller 3. close
   4. best 5. friendlier 6. kind
   7. most nervous 8. nicest
   9. more sensitive 10. smart
3. 1. Who is the nicest?
   2. Who is the laziest?
   3. Who is the youngest?
   4. Who is the shortest?
   5. Who is the most pessimistic?
   6. Who is the best looking?
4. 1. Bob 2. Carl 3. Bob
   4. Alan 5. Bob 6. Alan

Lesson 19

VOCABULARY

1. a blouse (W) a coat (-) a dress (-) a hat (B) a jacket (W) jeans (B) a shirt (M) shoes (W, M) a skirt (W) socks (B) a suit (M) a sweater (-) a swimsuit (G) a tie (M) nylons (W) sneakers (B) a T-shirt (B)
4. 1. I always wear white socks.
   2. My sister sometimes wears jeans.
   3. She often wears black nylons.
   4. Her brother never wears a hat.
   5. My children often wear red T-shirts.
   6. I never wear formal clothes.

GRAMMAR

1.

adjective	comparative
good	better
great	greater
late	later
big	bigger
lazy	lazier
formal	more formal

2. 1. expensive 2. old 3. bad
   4. thoughtful 5. great
   6. friendly
3. 1. I'm less tidy than my best friend.
   My best friend's less untidy than me.
   My best friend's more tidy than me.
   2. I'm more pessimistic than my brother.
   My brother's more optimistic than me.

My brother's less pessimistic than me.
3. I'm less polite than my sister.
   My sister's less impolite than me.
   My sister's more polite than me.
4. 1. John isn't as tall as his brother.
   2. His girlfriend isn't as young as he is.
   3. Bob isn't as popular as Carl.
   4. His father isn't as casual as he is. He's not as formal as his father.
   5. He isn't as pessimistic as his father.
   6. His mother isn't as thin as he is.

READING AND WRITING

1. A. most comfortable; B. best; C. most fashionable
   A and C are men; B is a woman.

Lesson 20

GRAMMAR

1. 1. g 2. d 3. a 4. f 5. b
2. *Possible Answers*
   How old are you? 25
   How much is it / does it cost? $35
5. 1. How fast can you go?
   2. How far is it? / How far is San Diego?
   3. How much is gas? / How much does gas cost?
   4. How long does it take to get to Tallahasee?
   5. How much is bed and breakfast? / How much does bed and breakfast cost?
   6. How long does it take by train from Las Vegas to Phoenix?
6. 1. How fast 2. How old
   3. How long 4. How tall
   5. How big 6. How much
   7. How often 8. How many

VOCABULARY

1. 1. set out 2. speed limit
   3. desert 4. mile
   5. gas 6. passenger

READING

1. It refers to her bicycle ride around the world.
2. Because she was not athletic or young. She wasn't a good cyclist and she didn't have a bike. She had no idea how to mend a flat tire and she hated camping, picnics, and discomfort.